Hiring, Onboarding, and Ramping Salespeople

Salespeople

The T.E.A.M. Framework

BY CORY BRAY AND HILMON SOREY

FOREWORD BY DAVID BLOOM

AFTERWORD BY JODI MAXSON

ISBN 13: 9781706730989

TABLE OF CONTENTS

FOREWORD

The evolution of modern sales is rarely sparked by a truly new idea.

Mobile phones didn't invent selling on the go, any more than CRM invented customer relationship management or dialers invented the cold call.

Sales onboarding is no different.

People have been looking to make sales reps better at their jobs ever since the first caveman sales manager got his first caveman direct report. We've just evolved.

First, we had sales methodologies. Then, a CRM. Then RevOps, sales training, proper coaching, and readiness programs specifically for go-to-market teams.

Now, it's time for sales enablement to takes its place where it belongs—a strategic business function that improves top-line revenue and bottom-line growth by maximizing sales rep profitability.

Rep profitability should be the north star for leaders in charge of making new hires successful. And the #1 way to do that is to reduce ramp time.

Don't get me wrong—every salesperson goes through some sort of period where they are getting up to speed. Zero to quota in sixty seconds or less is an insane pipe-dream. But, rather than cramming onboarding into a one or two week boot camp, we should design programs that reflect the experience of the reps that we're onboarding.

Now normally, forewords don't have graphs, but hey, I'm a maverick. Take a look at the graph in figure 0.1. Salespeople transition through what I call the J-curve—at first unprofitable for the business as they learn, and then delivering increasing value over time as they hit their sales milestones, like first activity, first meeting, first pipeline, first deal, first quota, and first consistent quota.

Figure 0.1: The J-curve for sales rep productivity

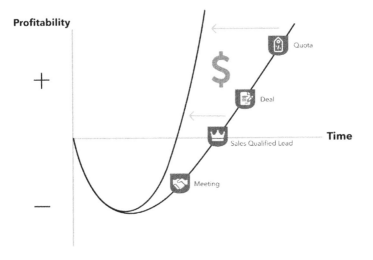

If our goal is to improve rep profitability, then we need to onboard and ramp faster. We need to cut the curve and shift the whole thing left, hitting each sales milestone sooner to achieve sales objectives earlier. After all, it doesn't take a rocket scientist to know that if salespeople find pipeline faster, they'll get their first deal faster. If they can book a meeting in week two instead of week three, they'll probably get to pipeline in week four instead of week five.

And if we can embed these milestones directly into programs, we can optimize those programs over time, giving teams a clear mandate for onboarding—**if a program isn't impacting the time to a specific milestone, then the program shouldn't exist.**

Imagine: instead of looking at vanity metrics like quiz scores and how much content gets consumed, what if we focused on the *outcomes* of our programs?

What if whoever's leading onboarding could definitively prove how much revenue the company realized for every dollar they put into their programs? Because I know one thing for sure—if they're going to get a seat at the table, they had better have the numbers more meaningful than certification metrics. No VP Sales ever walks into the boardroom and says: "Hey, great news! We all missed our number, but quiz performance is up 22%!"

No. If you want to be taken seriously, you need to move the metrics that matter and generate the revenue outcomes that executives care about.

Think back to the Kirkpatrick Model. For *years* we've been so focused on reaction and learning at the bottom that we've forgotten about the outcomes we're supposed to drive at the top: the behavior and results that matter most to sales leaders.

Salespeople want to know that their enablement team understands what it takes for them to be successful. They need to understand both the outcomes being driven, and that the outcomes being driven matter to them.

When we talk about outcomes instead of inputs and quotas instead of quizzes, I call it outcome-based enablement. It's the next evolution of the readiness function.

If we can tie program inputs to revenue outcomes, then hire, onboard, and ramp against those outcome success metrics, we can elevate the profession from a tactical component of the RevOps toolkit to a strategic business function that's critical to success. Management will finally have a *quantifiable* answer to the question 'Are my reps getting better, faster, and if so, why?'

This story will always start with hiring, onboarding, and ramping—and Cory and Hilmon have developed a complete strategic and tactical guide for leaders who are in the trenches. They explain not only what leaders should be doing in terms of onboarding and ramping to pivot the function toward real outcomes, but they get into the details of how to get it done.

Cory and Hilmon turn their countless consulting hours into an indispensable handbook on how to build a repeatable hiring, onboarding, and ramping engine—an engine that can (and should!) be an essential component of any growth machine.

Enablement isn't a new idea. Onboarding isn't a new idea. Helping salespeople be better isn't a new idea. But linking program inputs to the sales outcomes that executives actually care about? That very well might be.

David Bloom

1

INTRODUCTION

We developed the T.E.A.M. framework after having worked with hundreds of companies and thousands of salespeople, with the goal of providing a robust framework for organizations to attract, grow, and retain top talent.

Many sales leaders are adept at identifying talented candidates and successfully recruiting them, only to watch the dream fizzle as month six approaches and the individual has not yet attained quota.

Some managers can take a recent graduate right out of college, train and coach them into becoming a high-performer in their first sales role, only to have that sales rep stagnate and eventually leave due to a lack of professional growth, or readiness for the next opportunity.

Start-up founders frequently struggle to make their first sales hire. "Should it be someone I know? Someone who has a rolodex? Should I pay a fortune for someone with experience at one of the top companies? Should this person be more strategic or tactical?" Then, they realize months later that they have made the wrong decision, and it's back to square one, with increased pressure to get it right the second time.

Hiring, Onboarding, and Ramping Salespeople is the key to unlocking and applying the T.E.A.M. framework used by organizations—large and small—to drive repeatable growth, hiring rigor, accountability, and professional development. The framework includes the following components:

Talent Acquisition: Identify, interview, and hire the right people, at the right time, to achieve business goals.

Engage New Hires: Convert candidates to producers, quickly getting them up to speed and executing revenue-producing activities.

Accelerate Performance: Drive continuous improvement around competencies that lead to consistent results.

Mastery and Progression: Achieve mastery in the current role, and develop both strategic and tactical competencies for future positions.

All of the technology, data, systems, and product features in the world cannot replace the need for a consistently high performing team. Here's who will find value in this book:

CEO, COO, and Founder: Move from a reactive organization that grows unpredictably to a pro-active organization focused on the application of frameworks that drive repeatable success.

CFO: Understand the model for effective growth, and ensure that resources are not being squandered on ineffective programs, poor hires, or excessive staff.

Sales Leaders: Identify talent from larger pools, understand the target hire profile for each role, equip new hires for success, and drive continuous improvement.

Sales Enablement Leader: Overlay scalable and repeatable frameworks on the hiring process that allow for a metrics-based evaluation of the end-to-end process.

Customer Success Leader: Ensure that your team has the skills and motivation to perform across all areas of customer success, including driving upsells and renewals.

Sales Operations: Develop analytics to identify the success of new hires throughout their employment journey.

Evaluating Your Programs

Let's evaluate your T.E.A.M. approach to help identify the opportunities that this book can impact. Take the twenty-question quiz in figure 1.1.

Figure 1.1: T.E.A.M. approach assessment

Statement	Disagree	Somewhat	Agree
We struggle with inconsistent performance after salespeople are hired	☐	☐	☐
We struggle to hire people like our top performers	☐	☐	☐
We do not score candidates on their growth potential	☐	☐	☐
We use our "gut" when making hiring decisions	☐	☐	☐
We have lost good candidates due to a lack of execution (time, process, compensation)	☐	☐	☐
New hires struggle to ramp up quickly	☐	☐	☐
We are not able to hire for the core criteria needed for success	☐	☐	☐
Our hires struggle to grow into more senior roles	☐	☐	☐
We have positions open for a long time	☐	☐	☐
We have hired poor candidates who did not fit our culture	☐	☐	☐
We struggle to hire diversity of race, gender, cultural background, or experience	☐	☐	☐
We have lost good candidates to competitors	☐	☐	☐
We do not have a clearly outlined onboarding program beyond product training	☐	☐	☐
We cannot predict consistent results from a new hire once onboarded	☐	☐	☐
Onboarding consists of self-directed shadowing, review, and exploration	☐	☐	☐
We struggle to promote from within	☐	☐	☐
We lose or fire reps because they are unable to grow into bigger roles	☐	☐	☐
We do not have certification programs or evaluation criteria for skill competencies	☐	☐	☐
Our technology tools do not seem to be increasing performance	☐	☐	☐
We receive frequent requests from salespeople for new resources and applications	☐	☐	☐

If you marked "disagree" in every column, congratulations! You're in great shape! Please send us a message on LinkedIn and we'll happily refund the purchase price of this book. We mean that.

However, if you marked anything as "disagree" or "somewhat," you will receive an exponential return on the investment you made in this book.

A Word About Sales Enablement

We are strong believers in the role of sales enablement, as long as the enablement team is given the power and resources it needs to be successful. In our first book, *The Sales Enablement Playbook*, we outlined the role of sales enablement as a driving force creating a revenue-centric ecosystem inside of an organization.

With sales leaders focused on delivering monthly and quarterly results, the ability to have an enablement person or team with a long-term perspective and greater bandwidth to execute on these programs is key. CEOs often ask, "How do I position sales enablement to be successful?" Here's how:

> **They Must Have a Seat at the Table**: The head of enablement must be part of the leadership team, and not an assistant to the head of sales.

Remove Complexity: As Einstein said, "make things as simple as possible, but not simpler." This principle should be the guiding light of an enablement team as they weed out complexity and minutiae from the sales organization.

Hold Accountable to Metrics: Any enablement program must be designed to impact specific metrics, and leaders should have their compensation tied to specific performance criteria.

Drive Continuous Improvement: Status quo is not good enough. Nothing is ever "figured out," especially as a team scales in a changing market.

A strong enablement team can make all the difference as the frameworks in this book are put into practice. When we assess an organization's enablement effectiveness, it's a red flag when we discover that enablement reports to a sales leader and is responsible for running onboarding boot camps, but has zero influence in hiring and post-onboarding activities, or doesn't meet the criteria outlined above.

Our Use of Frameworks and Acronyms

Throughout this book, you will be introduced to important frameworks named with a relevant acronym.

To clearly illustrate why, let's look at two hypothetical salespeople, Frank Frameworker and Terry Tipstrick.

> **Frank** needs to fill three open roles on his team, and plans to use the H.I.R.E. framework. He will hunt for talent, create a structured interview plan, score people against a rubric, and evaluate the results of the hiring process.

> **Terry**, on the other hand, doesn't use a framework for hiring. He posts openings on free job boards, pulls available colleagues into the room for interviews, and bases his final hiring decisions on gut feel. When a new hire doesn't work out, he tries to figure out why and makes adjustments, sometimes.

The reality is that Frank and Terry can both be successful. However, when building a sales team, would you rather have each person running a consistent framework, or would you rather have an ad-hoc process with unclear outcomes driving the future of your organization's talent pool? Frameworks not only create more consistency, but they also make coaching easier and more impactful, as coaching ad-hoc activities are often challenging and have little lasting impact.

We're also asked about our use of acronyms, which we use when building frameworks. Here's why:

> Acronyms allow people to deliver a large amount of knowledge quickly (all one has to say is the term, and all

associations are brought to mind), to execute competently, and to communicate clearly and efficiently.

Acronyms should be relevant to the topic at hand. Made-up words that have nothing to do with the work being done cause confusion and are difficult to recall. As a result, you'll notice that we H.I.R.E. new employees, connect the D.O.T.S. for referrals, and in this book, focus on building a T.E.A.M.

By leveraging frameworks and acronyms, you will have simple and concise language that is easily understood by colleagues and has a depth of meaning that allows people to quickly get their point across without excessive narrative or interpretation.

How to Use This Book

If you have read our other books (Appendix A), you already know that our goal is to open-source sales knowledge based upon our success delivering consulting, coaching, and training to the fastest-growing companies on the planet. Throughout this book, we will outline the path to rolling out the T.E.A.M. framework within your company.

Throughout each chapter, diagrams are provided to reinforce topics covered in the text. Additionally, excerpts from other books we have written are included when the context is appropriate. You can find these images, excerpts, and more at HireOnboardRamp.com.

At the end of each chapter, we summarize the key points that were covered for an at-a-glance guide as you implement the T.E.A.M. framework.

As you progress through these pages, you will need to decide how thoroughly you will build out T.E.A.M. inside your organization. Avoid the temptation to do everything at once. Focus on the areas of immediate impact with the highest reward. Focus on building a strong foundation that drives results today, and then continue to improve over time.

Let's get started!

SECTION 1

Talent

TALENT ➡ **ENGAGE** ➡ **ACCELERATE** ➡ **MASTERY**

2

WHY START WITH TALENT?

Your talent strategy must be rock solid in order to build a team that consistently achieves its goals. Unfortunately, we often see organizations create an onboarding program without first evaluating their talent acquisition strategy and hiring frameworks. That's like trying to win a bake-off by messing with the oven temperature while ignoring your ingredients.

Figure 2.1: Talent market map (TMM)

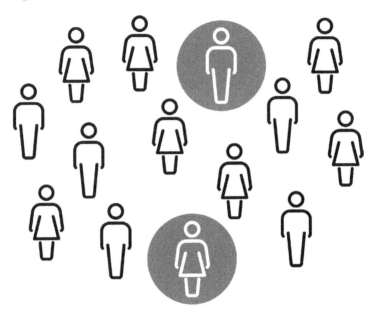

WHO ARE OUR NEXT HIRES?

Start-up founders and sales leaders are no doubt familiar with the term *total addressable market*, which is presented to investors to demonstrate the vast sea of buyers that represent potential revenue opportunity. Similarly, the *talent market map* (figure 2.1) shows the vast sea of potential candidates available to potentially work at your organization. Variables among this population of individuals that must be considered include compensation, experience, coachability, readiness, and interest.

The goal is to get the best candidate for your organization—not necessarily the best candidate available. What's the difference? The best candidate available will want the best compensation available. And he or she will deserve it. We've seen companies held hostage by "the perfect candidate" for great amounts of equity, hiring bonuses, astronomical salaries, personal massage chairs, and more. Seldom does the contribution to their new organization significantly outpace that of someone with less pedigree, and a strong commitment from the organization to develop them.

Unless you work at Facebook, Apple, Amazon, Netflix, or Google (also known as FAANG), chances are your pockets are not deep enough to continue to recruit from the pool of "the best available." No need. You can grow the best for you. If you find the right people and plug them into an effective system, they will excel and the organization will thrive.

Regardless, without the right talent, the other points covered in this book will be ineffective.

Chapter Summary

- A company's talent acquisition strategy is the foundation for building a successful team. Avoid overengineering onboarding programs if the talent strategy is not rock-solid first.
- A fundamentally sound and consistently improving talent strategy eliminates the need to overengineer onboarding programs.
- Find the *right* candidate for the open role within *your* organization instead of chasing the best possible candidate available, who everyone else is also recruiting.

3

TALENT COMPETENCY MODEL

Building a winning sales team requires identifying the specific competencies that *your* salespeople need to excel at, and evaluating your capacity to train new folks if they don't walk in the door with these competencies. The general categories under which competencies can be categorized for any role are *mindset*, *activity*, and *skillset* (figure 3.1).

Figure 3.1: Mindset, activity, and skillset

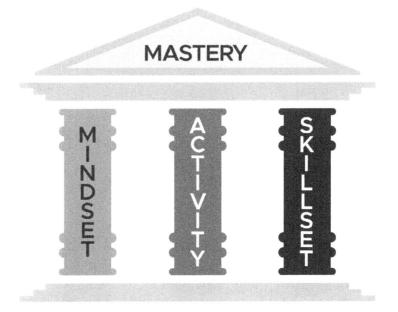

The competencies outlined in figure 3.1 position individuals to achieve MAStery of their domain. Once these competencies are defined for any given role, it's easy to identify an ideal candidate profile. Think of the competencies as criteria that are required to do a job well.

A candidate doesn't need to possess every competency when hired, but deficiencies should be well understood, and a training program should be in place to help fill the gap between where the person is today and where he or she needs to be to consistently perform at the desired level.

Management must be crystal clear on which competencies must be possessed by sellers and how each will be vetted during the interview process.

Figure 3.2: Competencies required for a job

Statement	Competency
Mindset	I uncover pain to become a trusted advisor
Activity	I use Linkedin to source 50 new contacts per week
Skillset	I use a framework to create next steps

Mindset

There are two types of mindsets, persistent and resistant, which we describe in *Coaching Salespeople*.

Excerpt 3.3: Persistent and resistant mindsets

> *The Persistent mindset is the voice in our heads that tells us "You can do it." For salespeople, this sounds like, "My product solves critical problems for CEOs" or, "By asking tough questions, I can save my time and my prospect's time," or "Of course prospects will reject me - they are busy and have been bothered by others. It's not a reflection on me or my abilities." The persistent mindset sets up a salesperson for success.*

The Resistant mindset is the other voice in our heads that tells us, "You're doomed! You're not gonna make it! You're going to fail!" For salespeople, this can sound like, "I know my product solves problems, but it's awfully expensive. I'm not sure it's worth that much." Or, "If I ask tough questions, the prospect is not going to like me," or "People keep saying no because I'm just not good at this." The resistant mindset protects us from difficult things (and simultaneously from growth) as a means of self-preservation. It resists that which is uncomfortable.

Failure to identify and coach toward persistent mindsets, and away from resistant mindsets, creates frustration between the sales rep and manager.

Prior to interviewing candidates, managers should identify which persistent mindsets are required to do the job well and which resistant mindsets will disqualify a candidate.

Paying close attention to the words candidates use is the key here. For example, a candidate might say:

> *"I think that sales technology has made the phone obsolete for reaching prospects."*

This individual is obviously going to be resistant to cold calling without some coaching.

Here is a more challenging example:

> *"Sales is a numbers game. You do the activity, and success follows."*

This statement is neither fact nor fallacy. It's simply a mindset. If your organization is one that is highly transactional, with a large volume and velocity of deals, it is a persistent mindset that will lead to success. However, if your organization builds wineries and sells one multimillion-dollar contract every four years, then the mindset is going to be a resistant one, because there may not be enough *numbers* to make the rationale resonate in the mind of your sales rep.

Activity

Activity is just as it sounds. What do your salespeople need to *do* to succeed? There are three categories of activity:

Type: The specific task that the salesperson will do, such as performing web-based demos, whiteboarding in person, or making cold calls to develop top-of-the-funnel prospects.

Quantity: The pure number of actions that need to be taken on a daily, weekly, and monthly basis.

Quality: The minimum bar that must be met for each action.

It's critical that candidates are willing and able to perform activity across all three categories, or else they will fail. The *company man* (how ridiculous does that sound now?) of generations past would "do what is needed for the company to be successful." Well, the person who fits that description today is the woman or man who has the most equity or highest title. No longer can we expect all employees to just grind it out for thirty years, especially when most salespeople have at-will employment agreements that allow their company to fire them at any time, with or without cause.

Gone are the days when someone can be hired and expected to do whatever the company needs. There is another kombucha-rator and snacks around the corner. Employees demand transparency and appropriate compensation for the jobs they are asked to perform.

Each employee's job description should be a living document that represents each person's current role and responsibilities. This way, there is never any ambiguity between the employee and management around what the role entails, and it creates a sense of fairness and stability. If part of the role *is* ambiguous, that's fine, and the appropriate language should be placed in the job description so all parties are on the same page.

The minute employees feel like they are being treated unfairly, which might include being asked to do work that they didn't sign up for or feeling like they are not being compensated properly, they will start considering alternative employment options. For top-performers, these options are many and easy to find.

If candidates have done a similar job earlier, it's fairly easy to determine if they are willing and able to perform the activity through the interview and subsequent reference checks. If they have not performed a similar job, hiring teams can find a parallel and identify whether they have the aptitude to perform the activity. Making a hiring commitment to someone who wants to do something they have never done before is a risky proposition for a manager.

Each activity required should also be spelled out in the job description. One mistake many companies make is to avoid discussing certain less-pleasant activities, either in the job description or during the interview process. We've heard great salespeople say, "what I'm doing today is not what was represented in the interview process." For example, if an account executive is responsible for sourcing 30% of their own pipeline, they should be told that. Will they be required to fly around the country to trade shows? Will they need to spend hours a week doing research, and then build campaigns to reach out to prospects individually in an account-based selling model? Or, is your company early-stage and you're not sure yet, thereby requiring your new hire to do some experimentation to figure it out?

Sales managers get frustrated when their team seems to be doing too little or too much activity. For example, too much research leads to prospecting reluctance, making it impossible to build the pipeline necessary to hit goals. Not enough research, on the other hand, creates the risk that activity is directed outside of an organization's target market. Mitigate these risks by having clear definitions in the job description and open discussions during the interview process. If someone doesn't want to do a bunch of online research or doesn't want to make cold calls, and these activities are required to be successful in the job, both parties are better off knowing before the hiring decision is made.

Skillset

In addition to having the right mindset and performing the right activity, one must possess "a certain set of skills" to succeed in their role. These skills fall into two categories:

Acquired: Cognitive, technical, and or interpersonal abilities already learned, applied, and validated through assessment or job performance.

Developing: The skills that have been (1) identified as job-critical and undeveloped as of today, and (2) have a clearly outlined path to attainment through training, coaching, or personal development.

The latter category is the area in which a company anticipates being able to make an impact through its systems, management, and process.

Industries that require top talent often use scouts to determine who performs well in each required skill area. Record labels use A&R and talent organizations to identify up-and-coming stars, then sign them and provide access to abundant resources to assist in them becoming the next big thing.

National Football League (NFL) teams do a great job of knowing both what skills a collegiate player will need to be successful as a professional, and assessing the current state of these skills in a fairly straightforward way. The NFL combine, an event held each year before the draft, puts players through a series of standardized activities to gauge their current acquired skills, and those that are developing.

Based on the outcome of the combine, players move up or down in the draft order. Sometimes skills in the developing category will doom a pro football career.

Similarly, any sales role should have a list of specific skills that must be present for success, and organizations must test for both acquired and developing skills.

A mid-market account executive who sells a B2B product with a sixty-day sales cycle that involves two-three different buyer personas might have the minimum and ideal skills that are outlined in figure 3.4.

Figure 3.4: Example skill matrix for a mid-market account executive

Skillset	Acquired	Developing
Discovery	Uncover sufficient pain to close a deal	Maximize deal size by uncovering pain from several stakeholders
Demo	Perform relevant computer-based demos	Conduct whiteboarding sessions to tie solutions to pain
Proposal	Craft a relevant proposal	Negotiate deals without management oversight
Leadership	Answer questions from junior colleagues	Formally coach junior colleagues

Chapter Summary

1. The three pillars required to achieve mastery are mindset, activity, and skillset.
2. Identify the competencies required for a job across each pillar prior to interviewing candidates.
3. Identify the persistent mindsets critical to success, and the resistant mindsets that should disqualify a candidate or require exploration.
4. Understand the type, quantity, and quality of activity required for salespeople to be successful in your organization.
5. Outline the skillset required for a successful new hire. Understand which of these skills must have already been acquired, and which can still be developing.

4

THE H.I.R.E. FRAMEWORK

The number one concern of CEOs in the most recent Conference Board Annual Survey is *hiring talent*; it's also the top concern of the entire executive suite.

Analyst reports, surveys, and news articles consistently state that chief executives view the lack of talent availability and skills as *the biggest threat to their business.*

In figure 4.1, we outline the talent lifecycle of a sales-hiring organization. Start-ups and small companies are typically able to fill talent pipelines with the leadership's network of friends and coworkers from previous companies. As these organizations grow, *dilution of proximity* begins. Organizations begin to rely on employee referrals, recruitment, and job postings to feed the talent pipeline driven by business demand, which poses challenges in the forms of quality and quantity. Most teams never leave this gerbil wheel of: business need => job requirement => recruitment efforts => hire.

Talent planning allows an organization to forecast headcount, identify stars early, benchmark against top performers, and source from a far more diverse pool. Here, the talent plan creates a consistent pipeline of ready, qualified, culture-fitted employees that can be effectively plugged into open roles.

Figure 4.1: The war for sales talent

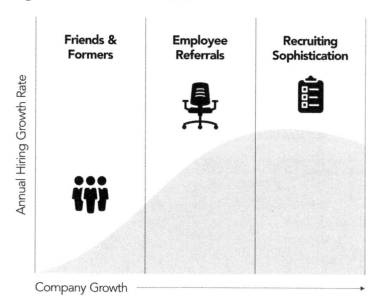

In this chapter, we cover the application of the H.I.R.E. framework to the talent planning process so that the right candidates become employees, and the wrong ones don't. The components of H.I.R.E. include Hunt, Interview, Rubric, and Evaluate.

Hunt

In competitive talent markets where perfectly qualified candidates are not knocking on your door, it's key to proactively identify and contact potential hires. Prior to reaching out to these folks, make a list of the attributes of an ideal candidate, and then turn this information into a formal job description.

The first step is to outline the experience that someone must have to be hired, and then define the values that either represent the ideal hire, or that disqualify someone from the job, as outlined in figure 4.2.

Figure 4.2: Experience rubric

Experience	Ideal Value	Disqualifying Value
Performance		
Methodology		
Prospect Personas		
Sales Cycle		
Years in the Role		

Elaborating on figure 4.2, experience could mean the following:

Performance: Quantitative indications of the person's performance track record. For junior positions, this metric might not be critical, but for senior sales jobs, it's key to know that a salesperson can consistently achieve their goals.

Methodology: If your company has a sales methodology, it might be important that the candidate either used the same one in the past, or at least that they are comfortable working within a sales methodology, as opposed to operating on an ad hoc basis.

Prospect Personas: If a new hire will be expected to sell to a certain persona, such as CFOs, candidates who have done so before will see faster results compared to those who have not. A salesperson who can speak a prospect's language and empathize with what they do all day is better positioned to succeed. Sellers who have no idea what prospects do often say things that trigger unspoken resistance, damage rapport, and result in lost opportunities.

Sales Cycle: If a new hire has never worked on a deal that took more than one meeting to close, managing a multi-touch, multi-persona sales process over the course of months is going to introduce a lot of new challenges.

Beyond experience, the compensation offered must attract qualified folks as well; otherwise, the candidate pool will be very small and hiring risk is increased.

When posting jobs in public, it's tempting to low-ball compensation to either try to find a good deal, or to avoid creating animosity internally around how much people are paid, but this practice often has the adverse impact of preventing the right candidates from applying. Companies end up paying more in the long run, and continuously endure unfilled positions, struggling managers, frustrated recruiters, and unmet goals. Ante up. If someone thinks they are worth $200k, they will not apply for a job that is listed at $140k, and the hiring manager will be stuck with trying to choose the best *unqualified* candidate for the job who is really worth only $100k, but has decided to "aim higher."

To quickly fill the talent pipeline with quality candidates, identify companies where the people with the attributes outlined in figure 4.2 work today, and begin recruiting. Avoid relying on the obvious big companies, as it is incredibly difficult to compete with deeper-pockets, amenity-rich environments . . . or even if you can, *everyone else* is already targeting these folks. Be creative and source from lesser-known strategic talent pools.

A word of caution: as your company becomes more and more successful, others are sure to use your team as their source of candidates to hire.

> *. . . the majority of people who took a new job last year weren't searching for one: Somebody came and got them. Companies seek to fill their recruiting funnel with as many candidates as possible, especially "passive candidates," who aren't looking to move. Often employers advertise jobs that don't exist, hoping to find people who might be useful later on or in a different context.*

> - Peter Cappelli, "Your Approach to Hiring is
> All Wrong," *Harvard Business Review*[1]

Beyond directly recruiting strangers, spend effort on getting warm introductions to potential hires who fit the profile outlined on the experience rubric. The D.O.T.S. framework from *Triangle Selling* is the best means of asking for referrals, and is summarized in excerpt 4.3.

Excerpt 4.3: The D.O.T.S. framework for referrals

Triangle Selling Framework: Connect the D.O.T.S.
Referrals are one of the best ways to find good prospects.
Our framework for generating referrals is D.O.T.S.:

Demographics: *What is the profile of the person to whom you want to be referred? Relevant attributes include the person's title, location, or industry.*

Options: *Where might a candidate be working today instead of working at your company?*

Traits: *What do strong candidates have in common? What do you know to be true about them that most people might not? What's your secret sauce?*

Symptoms: *What are the signs that a candidate isn't happy where they're at, but might be at your company?*

It's not necessary to use all four points of the D.O.T.S. framework. The key is to be specific so that the person being asked remembers the context and will recognize relevant candidates in the future. Complicated or verbose asks are quickly forgotten.

In the example below, Pat and Dottie are both employees at a small company that's growing fast and hiring salespeople. Here's what they're saying in an attempt to meet candidates:

> **Pat**: *We're hiring salespeople. It's really a great place to work. Let me know if you know anyone looking for a job, and I'm happy to talk with them to see if it might be a fit.*

> **Dottie**: *We're hiring B2B salespeople with 2-10 years' experience. Great candidates are frustrated by their current lack of growth opportunities and want to have a big impact at a small company. Let me know if you know anyone who might be a match.*

Pat's ask will quickly be forgotten, while Dottie's is more memorable since the demographics were specific (B2B and experience level), options were clear (continue working at the big company), and traits were as well (desire to impact a small company). Instead of simply asking if someone "knows anyone," connect the D.O.T.S.

Interview

Interviews are an organization's tool to determine if the candidate is as good in real life as they appear to be on paper. Unfortunately, most are conducted without adequate preparation, and vary from a useless pitch on the company to "sell me this pen." Interviews are where personal biases are most likely to show up, and companies end up making hiring decisions not based on who would be the best candidate, but instead hire people who the interviewers personally liked for a variety of reasons that may or may not relate to success in the role.

Structured interviews present apples-to-apples comparison, and either quickly identify top candidates, or result in rapid disqualification. The word "structured" in this context refers to the sequence of interviews, who is involved, and what is covered in each. A diagram showing a structured interview process is presented in figure 4.4.

Figure 4.4: A structured interview process

Stage	Interviewer(s)	Topics Covered
Phone Screen		
Chronological		
Experiential		
Reference Check		

Figure 4.4 shows that each interview belongs to a specific stage and has specific people who will be involved. The topics covered range from the high-level goal of the interview, down to the level of what questions the interviewer will ask and what types of responses to look for—good or bad.

The number and type of interviews that take place will vary depending on the role. These include familiar formats, such as phone screens, in-person conversations, experiential interviews, and reference checks. We are simply orchestrating these interactions across the interviewing team.

Consider the following interview structures:

Anne walks in for her in-person interview. The VP of Sales talks through her prior work experience, and then steps out to see who is free to interview next. One of the sales managers will be free in fifteen minutes, so a salesperson who happens to have gone to the same school as Anne is asked to chat with her for a bit. Fifteen minutes later, the sales manager walks in and talks through Anne's prior work experience, asking the same questions as the VP of sales did previously.

Brenda arrives for her in-person interview. The VP of Sales talks through her prior work experience. As they finish, a marketing manager walks in and takes over the interview, collaborating with Brenda on a data set to uncover her experience with key buyer personas. The final sales manager enters to take Brenda on a tour of the office, while focusing questions on how Brenda has successfully applied a sales methodology to yield consistent results.

The team using an unstructured interview with Anne didn't learn much, and the candidate didn't have a great experience. The team interviewing Brenda in a structured manner has beneficial data points across a number of single-focused individuals and has stress-tested key areas, such as selling to specific personas and leveraging a sales methodology.

Interviewer roles must be clearly defined as follows:

Observer: Is focused on neuro-linguistic programming (NLP) signals (such as eye movements), micro-expressions, and contextual signals.

Coach: Prepares the candidate for the experience (what to expect) and purposely provides guidance to uncover coachability.

Evangelist: Ensures that the candidate is presented with an accurate and encouraging view of the role and the organization. Also ensures that candidate questions are answered honestly and thoroughly, and that candidates have the opportunity to interact with the right team members to make an informed decision.

Aggregator: Is tasked with uncovering specific information in their interaction using *what, how, and why* questions.

Interviews should also be structured in terms of who does what, with whom, when, and how. Think of it like "blocking" for a play, where actors are strategically positioned for maximum impact in delivering the story and engaging the audience. Do not:

- Randomly grab "interview committee" members at the last moment.
- Usher a candidate from room to room with interviewers who are unprepared, or worse --- who ask the same questions.
- Involve anyone in the interview process who does not clearly add value.
- Involve anyone in the interview process who is not fully informed as to the rubric, criteria definitions, and scoring criteria.
- Waste a candidate's time with multiple interviews or interactions, both of which do not inform the candidate and the process.

Now, let's dig in and see how to apply structure across each stage of the interview process.

Phone Screen

The key with the phone screen is to replicate a real-life scenario that the candidate will face on the job. Salespeople are often speaking with prospects who are stressed out, in a rush, have higher priorities, and don't want to commit to the next step. The phone screen presents an excellent way to test how they handle high-pressure situations like these.

Observe the following exchange to see how a phone screen comes to life. Evaluation begins with the very opening of the conversation.

"Pat, I appreciate speaking today. I've got a few folks I'm talking with today and things are hectic as usual. I wanted to ask a few quick questions, and then based upon our conversation, I'll be deciding who we move forward in the interview process. OK?"

Evaluation:

- Maintains poise
- Demonstrates empathy
- Potentially asks clarifying questions (amount of time, an opportunity to ask questions, process?)

Warning Signs:

- Overly accommodating
- Demonstrates no awareness of urgency
- Gets flustered

Next, we look at relevance.

First Question: *"At a high level, can you walk me through two or three things in your background which you believe to be relevant to the position?*

Second Question: *"What are your long-term goals?"*

Evaluation:

- Concise
- Relevant previous experience
- High-value performance criteria

Warning Signs:

- Not following directions
- Lack of specifics
- Irrelevant narrative
- Regurgitation of job description or website

After relevance, we examine achievements.

"What have you excelled at in your previous jobs or academic career?"

Evaluation:

- Specifics
- Metrics or numbers
- Relevance to job

Warning Signs:

- Generalities

- Irrelevance
- Nebulous achievements

The next focus is weakness.

"What have you struggled with in previous jobs?"

Evaluation:

- Specifics
- Context

Warning Signs:

- Inability to answer
- Evasiveness
- Irrelevant functions

Now, start digging into specific sales skills.

"How would or do you go about getting conversations to convert to opportunities or revenue?"

Evaluation:

- Clear system
- Repeatable process
- Demonstrated understanding of human behavior

Warning Signs:

- "Artsy" answers
- "People close themselves" or other lack of control
- Theory without experience

The ability to talk about money is critical for success in sales, and this area is where we will dig in next.

"What kind of compensation are you looking for?"

Evaluation:

- Clarity and bravery
- Ability to frame without committing
- Questions asked
- Admission that it's awkward

Warning Signs:

- Evading the question
- No idea
- No backbone

Then we calibrate references.

"Who were the people who held you accountable? Who did you collaborate with? Who helped you grow?"

Evaluation:

- Names
- Clarity in growth opportunities
- Context

Warning Signs:

- "I can't remember"
- Evasiveness
- "I'm a perfectionist" answers

Take note of who they mention here, as these are the folks to ask about when it comes time to tee up reference checks.

Finally, the salesperson needs to close. It's not enough to ask them how they close or hear stories about how they've done it in the past; *they actually need to close*. This part of the phone screen is an example of an experiential interaction to gauge specifically how the candidate will react in a real-life scenario. More experiential situations will be presented later in the interview process.

> *"Well, that's all I've got, Pat. Again, I appreciate you getting on the phone. This afternoon I'll make a decision regarding who we bring in for interviews. If you don't hear from us, I want to wish you good luck with your search."*

Evaluation:

- Push back around criteria
- Asking questions about company and role
- Asking for evaluation of conversation
- Asking for next steps

Warning Signs:

- "Thank you for your time."
- Not following whatever they claimed they do in closing conversations
- Otherwise wilting

That's it! The entire phone screen takes thirty minutes or less and uncovers tremendous insight into how the salesperson will perform.

Contrast what you have read here with the time-wasting getting-to-know-you phone calls during which an interviewer talks about their own background, the company's history, and how awesome the team is.

Chronological

The chronological interview occurs after a candidate has passed the phone screen and ideally takes place in person or via video conference. Here, walk through the candidate's resume step-by-step, beginning with the oldest relevant position, then moving forward. Questions to ask for each position include:

- What job(s) were you hired to perform? What metrics were used to measure your activity? Your success?
- What do you think you excelled at? Tell me about a great win.
- Where did you struggle? Tell me about a deal that you consider a loss.
- Who were the people who held you accountable? Who did you collaborate with? Who helped you grow?
- Tell me about your working relationship with each of these people.
- What will each of them tell me you did well? What will they tell me we could support you regarding?
- What impact was made on the organization that can be attributed to you? How could you have made an even bigger impact?
- What caused you to leave that role or organization?

Experiential

The experiential portion of the interview further clarifies how the salesperson will actually perform, if hired.

For a sales role that will require sourcing leads, here is the place to give the candidate a specific persona to source, and a laptop and time frame in which to do so. If you want to add an additional data point, let's pretend you have a very busy sales floor. You have determined in your competencies development exercise that focus amid distraction is key. Someone who requires a meditative environment to get work done will not survive your gong-ringing, high velocity, open floor plan. Well, sit them out there with the rest of the team and ask a few select folks to go chat them up. Are they able to deflect, *"It's so good to meet you! I've got 10 minutes to finish this thing for Jennifer. Can I catch you after the interview to chat?"*

Or do they come back with a half-finished effort and an invite to happy hour? You'll have to get creative here, but the idea is not to "trick" the candidate or play silly games. The idea is to put them into a situation they are likely to encounter regularly and see how they perform.

Some examples we have helped define include:

Coachability: Have one interviewer advise the candidate to do something with the next. *"Brad is a numbers person. Please be sure to walk through your path to quota attainment with him."* Brad, of course, is fully aware that this instruction has been given and will create an opportunity for the candidate to demonstrate their ability to take coaching.

Prioritization: Provide three tasks that have a clear path to a specific outcome. Then allow a limited amount of time to complete. See what the candidate prioritized.

Collaboration: Have the candidate work with someone on the team who they may work with regularly on a small project.

Ability to Follow Instruction: Give some specific instructions (it can be as easy as where to find specific information online or as complex as how to complete a project) and examine the candidate's ability to get it done.

Demo: Ask the candidate to demo a product they are familiar with already.

Curiosity: Present the candidate with an opportunity to interview someone on the team. Evaluate the depth and relevance of the questions asked. Or, simply evaluate their curiosity throughout the entire conversation.

Rubric

Quantitative rubrics help hiring teams work together to identify the best candidate, while eliminating many of the biases that can exist in the hiring process.

Figure 4.5 shows an example where the company has determined the specific criteria to evaluate against and has provided each interviewer with the ability to score each candidate across each criterion.

Figure 4.5: An interview rubric

Skill	Interviewer 1	Interviewer 2	Average Score
Clarity	4	5	4.5
Curiosity	5	4	4.5
Closing	5	5	5
Coachability	6	5	5.5
X-Factor	5	7	6
Assessment Score			5
Average Score	**5**	**5.2**	**5.1**

The first four rows above should be self-explanatory, but interviews often fail to specifically assess each of these issues in a quantitative way. Interviewers frequently anchor to a handful of items that may or may not even be critical for the job, and judge candidates in an innate way. This is where personal bias seeps into the interview process and suboptimal hiring decisions are often made.

The x-factor is the place where "gut feel" is added. By letting each interviewer simply put down their opinion here, it forces them to also think critically across each of the other skill categories.

The assessment score, while listed as the final data point here, is ideally administered right after the phone screen to benchmark the candidate against others across a number of categories. The assessment also informs the interview process, thereby allowing the interview team to dig deeper into areas of concern or to get evidence of strengths.

Sales Skills Assessments

Most high-profile jobs require candidates to take assessments. The NFL combine we mentioned earlier includes the Wonderlic exam. Senior executives interviewing for positions in large corporations often take a battery of assessments that range from a personality focus to others that test their cognitive capabilities.

Sales teams that use assessments as part of their hiring process are at a competitive advantage over their peers, since they are able to objectively identify strong candidates, coach them effectively when hired, and weed out those who are not positioned for success.

There are three types of assessments that organizations tend to use:

Personality: These are tests like Meyers–Briggs that offer a panel of personality traits and the degree to which an individual expresses each. We see little value in these assessments for sales hires.

Behavioral: Assessments like DISC observe, describe, explain, or predict behavior. These assessments are great for understanding how an individual will work on a team, but do not indicate strengths or weaknesses related to how they sell.

Skills: These test the sales skills of a potential hire and provide insight into their opportunities for growth.

The skills assessment adds the most value to the talent identification process. While these assessments are not magic bullets, they are directionally accurate and can paint a picture of how much professional development an individual will need based on their current skill level. Some companies with smaller budgets for sales compensation tend to hire people on the lower end of the performance scale and invest energy in training to fill in the gaps surfaced by the assessment.

It's key to tailor the interview to the level at which someone performs on the assessment. Low performers should be interviewed in a way that tests their ability to be trained and coached, since they have a lot of *developing skills*. Candidates with strong assessment results should be interviewed in a way that examines how they will be able to apply their skills to the challenges of their role.

Evaluate

After the assessment has been completed, interviews are finished, and all interviewers have filled out their rubrics, it's time to evaluate the candidate and make a decision. The rubric for each interview should be consolidated into a master rubric, where the total score for each interviewer is assigned to each candidate, such as in figure 4.6.

Figure 4.6: A consolidated interview rubric

Candidate	Interviewer 1	Interviewer 2	Interviewer 3
Candidate 1	5.2	5.8	5.6
Candidate 2	6.1	5.9	6.0
Candidate 3	3.6	4.0	3.8

Immediately:

- Collect all completed rubrics following the interview
- Get all qualitative information *now*
- If you are going to continue the process with a candidate, let them know
- Debrief the interview efficiency and remedy any issues immediately

Reporting:

- All interviewers should be prepped to complete the rubric. The X-Factor exists specifically to allow for "gut" feelings, which may not fall into a specific criteria category.

- Is not done by committee in narrative
- Should be tallied and circulated to participants

Reference Check for Coachability

Reference checking is a critical part of the interview process for any sales hire. Here is guidance on teeing up references:

- Pick the bosses, peers, customers, and subordinates you have identified through the interview process. These must be the people a candidate mentioned when asked *"Who were the people who held you accountable? Who did you collaborate with? Who helped you grow?"*
- Ask the candidate to set up the reference conversation, which makes it much more likely of actually happening, and more importantly puts the onus on the candidate to chase people down. If the candidate finds it difficult to get these appointments set in a reasonable time frame, that's a red flag.
- The total list should be five to seven people

Reference questions to ask include:

- What was your working relationship with Jessie?
- What were things Jessie did better than most? Can you give me an example?

- What had you identified as some opportunities for Jessie's skill development? Can you give me an example why?
- How did she perform in a team setting? Any concerns having her lead or be part of a team?
- How would you rate Jessie's performance on a scale of zero to three, with three being extraordinary? Why did you pick that number?
- Jessie mentioned that her biggest professional gap is _____. Why do you think she said that?
- Given the chance, would you hire her again?

Hiring Retrospectives

Bad hires are inevitable. The best companies put energy into learning lessons from bad hires and attempting to tweak their process to mitigate the risk of repeating mistakes in the future.

Figure 4.7 outlines a hiring retrospective summary that should be completed once it's possible to make a determination as to how the process went. Bad hires can surface as early as their first week on the job, though it might take much longer. Certifying someone as a good hire is somewhat subjective, but quota attainment two quarters in a row without any negative impact on company culture is a reasonable metric.

Figure 4.7: Hiring retrospective summary

Category	Score (1=lo, 5=hi)	Comments
Performance	4	Strong, and developing well
Methodology	5	Great fit
Prospect Personas	4	Learns fast and is driven
Sales Cycle	3	Needs work to move to next level
Years in the Role	5	Works hard

Once the hire is scored, it either affirms that the hire was good and that the current process is working, or it indicates a weakness in the application of the hiring framework.

Chapter Summary

- Create a talent plan and leverage the H.I.R.E. framework to ensure that you can consistently and efficiently bring the right people into your organization.
- When Hunting for candidates, identify the ideal type of experience for your specific role, companies they might have worked at before, and leverage the D.O.T.S. frameworks for introductions.
- Utilize structured Interviews to create an apples-to-apples comparison between candidates, and ensure you eliminate bias and narrow focus on the right person for your role.
- Use Rubrics to standardize scoring across candidates. Create a rubric for each role that best reflects your ideal candidate profile.
- Sales skills assessments should be used to vet candidates, disqualifying those who do not meet the required level of competence, and using the output of the assessments to interview more effectively and to coach folks who are hired.
- Once interviews are complete, Evaluate candidates and complete reference checks. Keep in mind that the reference check is not a *gotcha!*, but rather an opportunity to better understand how to optimize the performance of a new hire.
- Conduct hiring retrospectives after new hires have been on the job for a while in order to continuously

improve your implementation of the H.I.R.E. framework.

Notes

Peter Cappelli. "Your Approach to Hiring Is All Wrong." Harvard Business Review, May 2019. https://hbr.org/2019/05/recruiting

5

"HIRING" INTERNALLY

Internal promotions present one of the best applications of using talent competency models. In the absence of a defensible competency model, employees typically tie their case for promotion to how many trips the Earth has made around the sun since they started their job. As a result, managers either give in and prematurely promote an individual, or give an indefensible "no," which leads to the rep getting frustrated and possibly dragging down team morale, or they find another job where the grass is invariably greener. It's also possible that there is then a mass exodus ("if it happened to my coworker, it will probably happen to me") of employees across the team.

Imagine the following scenarios:

> **Pat**, a mid-market account executive, has a one-on-one with her manager. During the meeting, Pat

says, "My one year anniversary is right around the corner. I think I'm ready for a promotion to the enterprise sales team, don't you?"

Taylor, also a mid-market account executive, has a one-on-one with her competency-driven manager. During the meeting, Taylor says, "My one year anniversary is coming up. I'm paying close attention to each of the goals I need to hit to earn my promotion. I think my weakest area right now is doing demos with both technical and non-technical stakeholders in the room at the same time. Do you think we can have a coaching session next week so I can make sure that I am on track for a promotion?"

The first scenario is where a lot of managers find themselves, faced with promotion decisions based purely on the amount of time that has passed since the employee joined the company. Sure, it's possible to come up with reasons why a promotion will or won't make sense, but without having communicated this rationale early and often, it's hardly fair.

The manager in the second scenario is in great shape. Expectations have been clearly set, and the salesperson is taking them seriously. Knowing that achieving mastery within certain competencies is the only way to move to the next level, the AE is focused on what matters.

Internal Promotion Structure

Companies with a strong internal promotion path have a competitive advantage. Modern employees yearn for the combination of upward mobility and job security that internal promotions provide. At the same time, organizations with specific revenue and profitability goals require talent stability in order to get to where they need to be in a predictable manner. Attrition is extremely disruptive.

The best promotion paths provide employees with a clear view of what their next role will be, a rough timeline on how long it will take to get there, and what must happen for the promotion to be offered.

Once the next steps are identified, the key is to demonstrate specifically what's required to get there. For example, figure 5.1 outlines an example of what a salesperson might need to do in order to move from a small business account executive to a mid-market account executive (AE).

Figure 5.1: Internal promotion requirements from small business to mid-market AE

Category	Statement
Quota Attainment	Attain quota in 3 of the last 4 quarters, with no quarter below 80%
Certifications	Pass the mid-market discovery and demo certifications
Professional Development	Present a lunch-and-learn to the team on a customer use case you have mastered
Culture	Have zero HR write-ups for behavior problems

Notice how figure 5.1 focuses on outcomes that are clearly indicative of success in a future role. Furthermore, with the ability to observe performance in these areas over a significant period of time, management can make confident assumptions regarding what to expect post-promotion. Hiring externally presents a number of risks here that can be partially mitigated through utilizing the H.I.R.E. framework, but nothing beats working with someone when vetting candidates.

Now, compare this structure to an organization that uses a time-based internal promotion structure, such as figure 5.2.

Figure 5.2: A time-based internal promotion structure (not recommended)

Role	Time to Next Promotion
Sales Development Rep	9 months
Small Business AE	1 Year
Mid-Market AE	2 Years

If the promotion structure in figure 5.2 has been promised to employees without any associated performance-based milestones, what do you think happens when the small business AE is coming up on their one-year anniversary in the role? In their mind, they are about to be promoted. If they have failed to consistently hit their quota, they likely still have justified the promotion to themselves based on the market, product, or pricing structure. Whatever happens, it is not a good situation for anyone when an employee thinks they should be promoted, the manager doesn't, and there was a lack of specific milestones and metrics put in place to gauge the eligibility of the employee.

Companies sometimes struggle for myriad reasons at various points in time due to forces outside of their control, such as fluctuations within the economy or their industry. Often, the promotion path is no longer viable, or temporarily not feasible. In our experience, if the employee still believes in the company and management's ability to execute, they will still stick around if they feel like they are being treated fairly and have certainty regarding the impact of adjusted expectations.

In times where there are more people ready to be promoted than there are roles available, there are a few things companies can do:

Create a Priority List: Promote the people who have the best key metrics, such as performance vs. quota, and make sure that the calculations behind this list are transparent to everyone.

Accelerate Commissions: Pay out a higher commission rate above a certain level of quota attainment. Each dollar sold beyond a salesperson's quota is highly profitable to the company, since the salesperson's base salary and overhead expenses have already been covered by attaining quota. As a result, paying a higher commission rate will still result in a higher level of profitability to the business, up to a certain point.

Equity Grants: Provide the employee with "golden handcuffs" in the form of a fresh equity grant that vests over time.

To Fast-Track, or Not?

One common challenge is when there is an exceptional candidate who wants to move to the next level, but has not met some minimum criteria for an internal promotion. Maybe they have a lot of relevant experience and are succeeding at a pace well ahead of their peers. Maybe they work really hard and put in the hours that others are unwilling to commit. Or, it's possible that they're exceptionally intelligent and learn quickly. In any event, they might think they deserve the nod faster than others.

Companies that are not willing to accept fast-tracks often leave some of the best talent out of their ecosystem, either by not being able to hire them in the first place, or by prematurely washing out high-potential employees who may think their career paths are being slowed.

On the other hand, having rigorous exceptions for Toni but not Dennis can come across as playing favorites.

The decision to fast-track should be made on a company-by-company basis; if it's allowed to happen, very clear criteria must be in place around both competency mastery *and* performance.

Premature Promotions

Promoting people prematurely can be devastating, as any of the following situations might ensue:

Employee Failure: It's important for employees to understand that temporary setbacks are a part of the learning process, but there must be a clear path to success. Premature promotions often result in the employee having skillset and mindset deficiencies so serious that there's a real risk that they can't attain their goals. If there is a risk that internal hires are not ready, organizations need to either double down on enablement of existing teammates, or consider a class of external hires.

Team Misses: Individual failures increase the probability that the entire team goal is missed. With a team miss, both the employee and the team are in a precarious position, and unless the employee has been up leveled to the point where they can hit the goal next period, there is no clear path to success.

Cultural Deterioration: Promoting someone who isn't ready for a role can hurt culture in a variety of areas. First, people already on the team they are promoted to become frustrated by the new weak link. Second, people on the team from which they have been promoted now expect more rapid promotions, thus compounding the weak-link issue if it's not addressed. Finally, if the promoted employee washes out, it might seem like there's no clear career path for people, which can turn folks off who are looking for rapid career progression.

Putting the frameworks from this book into place and consistently adhering to them mitigates the risk that premature promotions even happen.

Chapter Summary

- Create and convey a clear internal promotion path for new hires that is transparent and fair.
- Set expectations regarding any circumstances that would forestall promotion opportunities including funding, business cycles, and market conditions. Consider in advance the criteria that would allow for an individual to be fast-tracked for promotion, and ensure that other employees view this process as fair.
- Avoid premature promotions, as they can lead to employee failure, team misses, and demoralization.

SECTION 2

Engage

TALENT ➡ **ENGAGE** ➡ **ACCELERATE** ➡ **MASTERY**

6

WHY ENGAGE, AND NOT "ONBOARD"?

Much is written about the "onboarding" process for new hires. It's not enough to bring folks onboard. They need to engage with tools, process, colleagues, playbooks, customers, and your system . . . then start rowing. Getting onboard is easy, so throughout this book, we will rarely use the word "onboarding," but rather focus on engaging the employee out of the gate, and then accelerating them toward mastery.

Figure 6.1: Simply onboarding doesn't accomplish much

Engagement involves equipping a new hire with all of the training, tools, and frameworks to begin to develop MAStery (Mindset, Activity, Skillset) in their role. In this book, we define engagement as all activities that start with a new hire being presented with their offer letter, up until they make their first meaningful prospect-facing activity (such as conducting a discovery call with a prospect in their target market).

Figure 6.2: The engagement phase

To create engagement, and not just check some "onboarding" boxes, concepts learned must be applied quickly. Salespeople will forget what is learned in the classroom if they are not able to apply their new knowledge and skills in real life right away, and even if they remember concepts in part, they will forget key details quickly. Furthermore, they won't trust what they learn unless it can be applied and results attained.

Too many organizations have concentrated "onboarding boot camps" where they super-saturate new hires' brains with impertinent information. This process is confusing and demoralizing. Tons of new materials have been introduced—none of which are applicable to the hire's immediate selling scenarios.

The greatest success is found when newly hired sales-people can apply what they have learned, make mistakes, ask questions, try again, and eventually get it right. *Apply* doesn't mean that they must effectively manage make-or-break meetings with your most valuable prospects. Instead, they need to get repetitions where they practice key skills required for the job either during internal role-plays or low-risk prospecting activities, such as inviting people to webinars or marketing events.

Chapter Summary

- Getting an employee onboard is easy. Engaging them and accelerating them toward mastery is the hard part—and the part that creates consistently high-performing teams.
- The engagement phase begins with an employee receiving their offer letter, and ends when they conduct their first meaningful prospect-facing activity.
- Concepts presented to a new hire but not applied quickly will be poorly applied—or worse, forgotten.

7

COLLABORATIVE AND SOCIAL RAPPORT

Human beings are social animals. As we mentioned earlier, gone are the days when a paycheck alone created a productive relationship between company and employee. Salespeople have many options today, and the workplace is now a place for personal development, professional development, social engagement, and, in some cases meals, snacks, kombucha, and dry cleaning! The goal of the engagement phase is to get new hires past their comfort zone to the point where they are receptive to coaching, expansion, and growth.

People change their behavior based upon one of two primal urges, which are to minimize threats and maximize reward. Also known as:

Pain: The need to avoid a threat or loss

Reward: The need to seize an opportunity

Years ago, management theorists would write epics about strict accountability, reporting, and top-down management. That alone just doesn't fly anymore. Managing today's employees through a series of "Pain" incentives will create a toxic environment with little retention, growth, or willingness to take the risks to develop master.

Understanding these motivations, however, presents a roadmap for leadership to create an environment in which a new hire can thrive. Trust is essential in developing this relationship.

In leadership training sessions, we discuss the benefits of establishing rapport, a trusted relationship with sales reps. The responses we receive from clients when asked "What happens when an employee trusts us?" include the following:

- They are more transparent about their challenges
- They seek our advice and counsel instead of hiding
- They keep their commitments
- They collaborate freely with their peers
- They are willing to take risks, even if they are uncomfortable
- They bring curiosity and passion to their roles

- They refer their friends and former coworkers to our company
- They don't play toxic games
- They give us honest feedback

It's easy to understand the value of rapport on a sales team. The challenge for management is to understand how it is established, maintained, and measured.

Neuroscience: The S.C.A.L.E. Framework

Dr. David Rock, author of *Your Brain at Work*, published a paper titled "A Brain-Based Model for Collaborating with and Influencing Others" in the *NeuroLeadership Journal* in 2008[1]. The paper was the result of interviewing over thirty neuroscientists, and the framework identifies the approach–avoid response as a means of influence and presents the key "social domains" or "drivers" impacting human behavior.

We have adapted this study to the application of rapport building using the acronym S.C.A.L.E.: Status, Certainty, Autonomy, Likeness, and Equity.

Figure 7.1: S.C.A.L.E. measures rapport

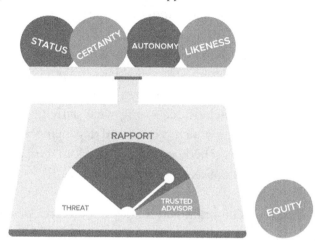

Status: An individual's perception of where they are in relation to their peers. When people experience a drop in Status, brain networks light up in the same way as if they have experienced physical pain. A perceived increase in Status lights up networks more significantly than if they have been given a monetary reward. A perceived drop in Status induces a response akin to if an individual has been physically attacked.

Certainty: Dr. Rock says, "The brain is a certainty-creating machine, always trying to predict what is going to happen." Certainty moves people toward reward, so salespeople must let buyers know what is going to happen next. When management provides clear expectations, they create Certainty, which allays fear and builds confidence.

Autonomy: When people feel they have no choice or control, they are stressed. Many folks choose sales because of the autonomy the profession provides, which includes choosing what activities to focus on during which part of the day, being able to dictate one's schedule, and the freedom to manage conversations as a salesperson sees fit.

Likeness: The brain automatically perceives new people as a threat. Humans naturally feel initial discomfort. The oxytocin response comes from effective rapport building. Note that it is Likeness that people are striving for here. Likeness enhances the perception of friend versus foe. Rapport actively creates common ground. Reinforcing the reason you have hired an individual and then integrating them into their workflow by focusing on the familiar (competencies, colleagues, industries, etc.) creates an opportunity for immediate Likeness and establishment of rapport.

Equity: Equitable exchange activates reward circuitry. Unfair exchange activates a danger response. In *How the Mind Works*, neuroscientist Steven Pinker[2] shares that this need for fairness emerged as an evolutionary advantage. In the hunter-gatherer days, when protein sources were unreliable, a large animal might have been more than enough meat for an individual, and it could be traded. Obviously, to be an effective trader, one needed to be able to detect deception or broken promises. So equity detection became an evolutionary advantage. In our world, once Equity is achieved, coaching becomes effective, accountability can be expected, and there is no grousing on the sales floor.

Managers should keep these drivers in mind at all times when planning and interacting with new hires and the existing sales team. When assessing team effectiveness, we often find that managers are "stuck" simply because they are failing to satisfy one or more of these drivers.

Rapport Stages

Keeping in mind that rapport is a state that is sought to be established, maintained, and then grown, the following sections outline how rapport maps to the four elements of the T.E.A.M. framework.

Talent Identification

Increasingly, data science is being leveraged to create omniscient managers armed with information including assessment psychographics, activity data, mock demos, references, relationship networks, and more. All this information is awesome, but it can be a bit overwhelming.

The amount of data available to a hiring manager today can also create a false sense of confidence, leading them to think, "I know this salesperson. I know their challenges." Keep in mind that the importance of these data is to be able to ascertain how the individual can *best be supported to optimize their impact inside of an organization.* It is not intended to be an episodic evaluation. Rapport at this stage is developed by demonstrating a commitment to the application of an individual's acquired skills and a path toward developing skills.

Engagement

Engagement begins upon acceptance of the offer letter. The orientation is the process of initial engagement and setting expectations. Important steps include:

- Creating clarity around the job and activities that the seller will perform
- Outlining the path to success for the salesperson
- Ensuring that the new hire knows what resources are available, and how to get help when they're stuck

Note that the goal is to focus on establishing and maintaining rapport by using the S.C.A.L.E. drivers, not about becoming best buddies. This is not about lunches, dinners, drinks, or fantasy football leagues. These "relationship-building" activities are fine; just don't mistake them for the science around which rapport is established to allow for a sales process to be effective.

Acceleration

Acceleration is a collaboration between salesperson and manager. It is not a confrontation or an adversarial construct but, instead, should look like the following:

- Complete certifications and receive additional training and coaching as needed
- Execute the sales process (for the mutual benefit of the organization and the salesperson)
- Consistently perform to expectations (keep meetings, accomplish what was intended, and maintain mutual accountability)
- Create opportunities for team collaboration while maintaining rapport and engaging new contributors from the organization

Mastery

This phase is the most important part of the rapport-building process, where the manager ensures that trust is ongoing.

- Continue to set clear expectations for measuring success
- Define an ongoing communication framework
- Lay the groundwork for future opportunities within the company
- Develop and manage toward growth plan

At this point, the manager and the salesperson are teammates, working together within their own roles toward a common goal. The stronger the teamwork, they faster the salesperson will achieve mastery.

Signals That Rapport Exists

Rapport might sound like an elusive concept, but there are some clear signals that it exists, including when the salesperson:

- **Trusts the manager's coaching**: When sales-people willingly attempt to implement coaching or training feedback.
- **Asks for advice**: When the salesperson seeks advice on issues that are not remedial. That's a great sign!
- **Provides referrals**: If the salesperson introduces potential new hires to the company, rapport has likely been built.
- **Tells the truth**: When a salesperson refrains from sugarcoating failures or challenges.
- **Does what they say they are going to do**: When salespeople keep their commitments.

Keep in mind the high cost and massive amounts of energy associated with recruiting a new salesperson. This investment can be blown by onboarding a new hire and then leaving them to their own devices. It can be equally squandered by neglecting to maintain and build rapport with tenured reps simply because they seem to not require as much attention. You better believe that a competitor is already sending your top performers love letters and trying to recruit them away.

Monitoring Rapport Levels

Pilots fly by monitoring their instruments, and when working in teams, managers should do the same. When having conversations with sales reps, monitoring the rapport meter is critical to ensure that the salesperson has not stepped into dangerous territory where rapport and trust start to erode. Signs that rapport is dropping to unacceptable levels include:

- A decrease in engagement
- An increase in hostility as the salesperson responds to coaching
- More guarded answers over time
- Broken commitments

In monitoring rapport levels, simply run through the S.C.A.L.E. drivers to determine what may be threatened. Then endeavor to fix the rapport issue before plodding ahead with your sales process.

Chapter Summary

- People change their behavior based upon one of two primal behavioral urges: minimize threats and maximize rewards. Management by threat is, thankfully, a thing of the past.
- The S.C.A.L.E. framework measures rapport by outlining five drivers: Status, Certainty, Autonomy, Likeness, and Equity.
- Management must be mindful of the growth of rapport across the four elements of T.E.A.M.
- By monitoring rapport levels, managers are certain to avoid an erosion of trust.

Notes

David Rock. "SCARF: A Brain-Based Model for Collaborating with and Influencing Others." NeuroLeadership Journal no. 1 (2008), https://www.epa.gov/sites/production/files/2015-09/documents/thurs_georgia_9_10_915_covello.pdf
Stephen Pinker. How the Mind Works (New York: W. W. Norton & Company, Reissue edition, June 2009).

8

ENGAGEMENT GOALS

The best way to engage new hires is to identify specific metrics to be achieved, and then track how salespeople go about driving success toward these metrics. Some metrics are binary, such as completing a session on product training, whereas others are not, and assess the quality of the new hire's discovery questions on a scale of one to three.

Engagement goals should be tied to specific "jobs-to-be-done." If you have read our other books, you know we are a big fan of professor Clayton Christensen's jobs theory, where he looks at the specific jobs that people are doing at a granular level, which eliminates a lack of understanding that comes with thinking in high-level abstraction.

Figure 8.1: Engagement must align with jobs-to-be-done

Job	Engagement Activity
Ask discovery questions	Craft and role play the delivery of discovery questions
Have pain-based conversations with CFOs and controllers	Learn what CFOs do, their pain, and how the salesperson's product or service solves the pain
Craft demo flows that relate to acute pain that was previously uncovered	Practice creating relevant demos based on pain that was uncovered during discovery
Consistently have next steps on the calendar	Learn the sales process and what next steps should be prescribed to the prospect after each type of interaction

Notice how the activities in the job column in figure 8.1 are very specific? It's tempting to say that a salesperson should be able to run a discovery meeting and present a compelling demo, but these instructions are too abstract for a new hire to take action, and not specific enough for management to identify and coach around key weaknesses.

During the first few days of a salesperson's job, they only need to be given the specific training and access to systems that they need for accomplishing their core jobs. Anything else distracts from what they should be focusing on at the time and will result in muddied expectations, lack of accountability, and excuse-making. Consider the following example from early on in the tenure of two employees:

> **Debbie** is trained on discovery. She practices discovery with her peers. She receives feedback on

her discovery techniques from her boss. She then gets a list of "practice leads" and schedules time with them to conduct discovery calls in order to demonstrate her skill prior to calling folks in her target market. Her calls are then reviewed by her manager and she's coached on how to improve.

Polly is also trained on discovery, but before she can practice it with peers, management, and prospects, she is first trained on the proposal development process, discounting procedures, and how to hand-off a newly signed deal to the customer success team.

Who will find early success? Debbie will develop strong discovery skills out of the gate, and then need some help with logistics when it comes time to close a deal. Polly, on the other hand, might not ever get to that point due to her surface-level introduction to discovery.

Chapter Summary

- Create specific, measurable goals for the engagement phase.
- Ensure that activity is broken down to the job-to-be-done level so it can be well understood and coached.

9

OFFER LETTER TO FIRST ACTIVITY

When it comes to engaging salespeople, your new hires will get out of the program what you put into the program.

This chapter outlines the components of a world-class engagement phase. Depending on your business, the items you include, the order and depth in which they are covered, and how they are delivered might vary.

The Offer Letter Sets the Stage

Until someone receives their first big promotion, odds are that the moment they receive an offer to work at your company is the most excited they will be about their job. As a result, it's important that leaders take advantage of this enthusiasm and use it to begin engaging the new hire.

This enthusiasm comes with the willingness to dig in and do some pre-work, which can relate to their role either directly or indirectly.

Direct pre-work might be becoming acclimated with your company's sales playbook, for example. This way, they will walk in on day one and have a very clear understanding of the key resource that they will use to drive quality activity during their first days on the job. If your company doesn't have a sales playbook that the team uses consistently to drive revenue, we have included an overview of what a great playbook looks like in figure 9.1.

Figure 9.1: An overview of a complete sales playbook

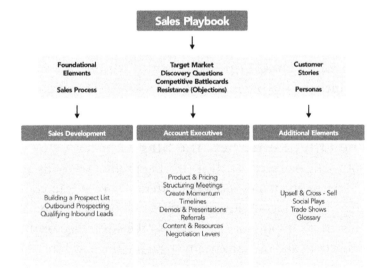

Indirect work might include reading books. We have seen great success when sales development reps (SDRs) are given the book *Sales Development* and have a firm grip on the basics. Also, if your sales methodology is open-sourced in a book format such as *SPIN Selling* or *Triangle Selling*, have the new hires read these prior to starting their job to get the lexicon down before day one.

Spaced repetition is critical for learning comprehension. Allowing people to have time between repetitions increases the chances that they'll remember what they've read.

Get HR Paperwork Done

Another way to create momentum with new hires is to ensure that HR paperwork is done prior to their first day. Imagine the following two scenarios:

> **Patrick** shows up on day one and is sent to HR to fill out his payroll, health insurance, and 401k forms. He then is directed to sales operations, where he signs up for several software products that he will use in the coming weeks.

> **Michael** shows up on day one, having done HR paperwork on Sunday night, and is doing discovery role-plays with peers within ninety minutes of showing up at the office.

Who wins? Michael, all day. It's a no-brainer to get the non-revenue-related activity out of the way so the salesperson can focus on what he or she signed up to do.

Create an Engagement Activity Backlog

In product management, there is the concept of a "backlog," which indicates all the tasks that need to be completed, by whom, and by when, in order to ship a product to customers. The goal with new hires is to build an activity backlog of everything that needs to happen to take someone from signing an offer letter to their first activity.

This backlog then becomes the engagement plan. The plan should be modular like Legos, so that each component can be customized for employees in different roles. If something isn't required for the first conversation with a prospect, consider deprioritizing it until later. The following list includes common prerequisites that must be covered during the engagement phase, prior to having a salesperson begin their core duties:

- Understand their target market, including the attributes of their ideal customers, as well as the types of prospects that should be disqualified out of the gate
- Become familiar with key buyer personas, including what these people do, their relevant pain, and how the salesperson will win with each

- Develop pain-based discovery questions to be used when talking with prospects
- Learn a couple of customer stories that can be used as social proof to make conversations more relevant
- Functional CRM training that demonstrates the minimum competence someone would need in their first couple of weeks
- Gain comfort navigating the sales playbook, so all the items that are not yet learned can be discovered when needed and put into action
- Practice responding to questions where the answer is unknown to ensure that the seller has strong conversational acumen

With these skills mastered, a salesperson is ready to start having conversations with prospects. Unfortunately, many organizations subject salespeople to a laundry list of what we call *the initially unimportant*, which includes:

- Product mastery
- Every custom field and integration in the CRM
- User training for every piece of sales technology
- Responses to every objection they have ever heard
- Demo decks for every circumstance
- Administrative tutorials (proposal creation, document signing, etc.)
- And much more . . .

When it's finally time to put this information to use, it's long gone from memory or has no context. Alternatively, we've seen companies run an "onboarding boot camp." Weeks upon weeks until they really do learn everything, at which point the hungry newly-hired salesperson has been turned into a professional student who will have a much lower "figure-it-out-factor" and lower resilience after failing than if they would have been brought into the organization the way we outline in this book.

Customize Engagement

Treating all people equally as they initially engage is a recipe for disaster. Different folks should have different tracks, depending on their job description and their current ability to do that job. It sounds overwhelming, but the hidden costs of forcing all new hires down the same track will show up quickly and will linger over time.

Figure 9.2 shows the bored-learning-lost framework that we first introduced in *The Sales Enablement Playbook*. In group training, people are in one of these three states, and some folks move from state to state over the course of the session. If you are able to level set the group, you can maintain the optimal learning state.

Figure 9.2: The bored-learning-lost framework

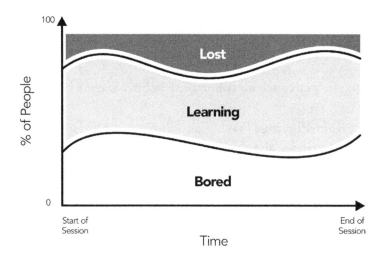

Group Training: The Ugly Truth

Companies that have not dedicated sufficient resources to engage new hires often have them either spend time in "onboarding tracks" that are not relevant to them, or fail to expose them to the specific competencies needed to do their job well.

Cohorts

Grouping new hires into cohorts helps accelerate engagement through peer-based learning, and also lightens the load on both managers and the sales enablement team. Bringing people from different backgrounds together with the common goal of preparing for success in their new roles is a powerful process, and learning will happen much faster as the new hires will make observations and see paths to success that might not be readily apparent to folks who have been working within the organization for a while.

Specific places where cohorts are helpful include:

Role-Playing: Having an existing employee bear the load for all role-plays is taxing. Computer-based role-plays help to a certain extent, but still, require existing employee resources to review them and give feedback. New hires can frequently iterate on role-play execution together, and then come back to management for a final stamp of approval.

Playbook Improvement: New hires are much more likely to see holes in the existing playbook, and are well-positioned to strengthen it for future classes of hires.

Executive Access: Incorporating executives from across the team is a great way to train and motivate new hires. For executives, working with cohorts instead of individuals reduces the strain on their limited bandwidth.

Cohort design should also consider the prior experience of the new hires. Putting veteran salespeople through sales 101 is going to quickly drain the energy and momentum that they had coming into the job. Conversely, putting junior hires into advanced sessions that are over their head might be interesting to them academically, but they will be challenged to grasp practical knowledge they can apply later on.

Deliver to a new hire specifically what they need at the right level, and they will be highly engaged.

Chapter Summary

- Leverage the enthusiasm that comes with starting a new job to begin engaging the salesperson before they arrive for their first day.
- Create a backlog of engagement activities and ensure that only those activities that are immediately relevant and will soon be applied are queued.
- Customize the engagement phase based on the needs of the new hire. Remain mindful of the bored-learning-lost framework for each participant. Create cohorts of new hires to improve the efficiency and effectiveness of new hire engagement, while also minimizing new hire-related interruptions on the existing team.

10

ENGAGEMENT CONTENT

Content to engage new hires might appear in the form of documents on a drive, information in an online portal or wiki, meetings, or ideally, an interactive sales playbook. A simple rule to remember is:

> *Engagement content should only be included to build competency around a specific job-to-be-done. If that is not the case, the content should not be presented to the new hire.*

Too many organizations flood new hires with *content they should know,* only to realize later that they didn't retain any of it.

Use What You Have

As we said in *Sales Playbooks: The Builder's Toolkit,* don't let perfection become the enemy of good.

For each new cohort of salespeople, allocate a time budget across the sales organization to work on content. The budget should be broken down into two categories: developing new content and refactoring what currently exists. Then, prioritize content projects using the Eisenhower Matrix (figure 10.1).

Figure 10.1: The Eisenhower matrix for content development

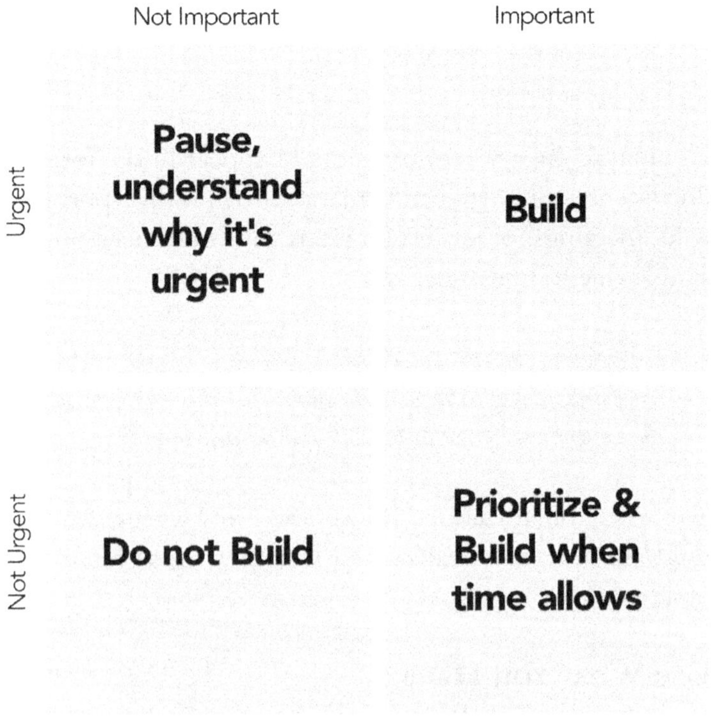

	Not Important	Important
Urgent	**Pause, understand why it's urgent**	**Build**
Not Urgent	**Do not Build**	**Prioritize & Build when time allows**

Ideas that lead to the development of content might come from:

Prior Cohorts: If people from the last cohort of new hires struggled at a certain point along their engagement and acceleration journey, make adjustments so the next cohort is better positioned for success.

Market Changes: If competitors or customers have evolved in a material way, update content so that new hires are prepared when confronted with these changes in the market.

Product Launches: Include any relevant information around new product launches. Maintain that the focus is on solving pain, and not all of the cool features that your company offers.

New Hire Attributes: If your next cohort will be more senior or more junior than previous new hires, make adjustments accordingly. More junior folks tend to need to learn a lot during their first few weeks, while experienced hires must focus on applying what they know in the context of your company.

Day One

Start with a bang. Your new employee will arrive with high energy, and it's management's job to maintain that energy for as long as possible. Constant constructive tension that creates urgency is critical during a new hire's first several weeks on the job. The longer this urgency remains, the faster they will get to their expected level of performance.

As with anything new, there will be challenges. Make it clear on the first day that the new hire will fail at some things, and failure is expected as they learn. In fact, a key attribute of the engagement phase should be that it creates the opportunity for the new hire to try, fail, and learn, as quickly as possible. Think about how the human body survives in a germ-filled world. Parents don't completely isolate children their entire lives so that they never contract an illness. The only way for a body's immune system to get stronger is to get sick, fight the sickness, and develop a tolerance. Fail forward fast.

Instructor-Led Sessions

Instructor-led sessions are a great way to engage new hires, as long as they are structured properly and there is adequate reinforcement. Live sessions allow employees to absorb information, while also being able to ask clarifying questions and role-play whenever possible. As a result, they are more likely to retain what they are learning and it's more likely to make sense.

When planning an instructor-led session, we suggest creating a checklist, such as the one presented in figure 10.2.

Figure 10.2: New hire training session checklist

Confirmed?	Topic
☐	The learning outcomes of the session are well-defined
☐	The activity within the session supports the defined learning outcomes
☐	The learnings from the session will be put into practice in the next 48 hours, or will be revisited in a future session to minimize forgetting
☐	The session is designed to be engaging, so people will pay attention
☐	Follow-up activities have been scheduled to reinforce learning

The absence of such a checklist often results in one of the following scenarios:

Death By PowerPoint: The presenter drones on while flipping through seemingly endless slides.

Enter-trainment: The audience is engaged and having a good time, but they're being entertained, not learning anything that can be applied, measured, and retained.

Neither one of these options is good. They don't have an impact, and while the latter often gets strong reviews coming out of the session, salespeople ultimately don't get what they need to be successful.

Beyond the general structure of the session, there are various attributes of strong in-person training sessions that maximize the probability that new hires will be able to apply the knowledge learned once they start working with prospects. Some techniques to make these sessions impactful include:

Get Everyone Talking: Out of the gate, have everyone in the room say something. Even if they are just exchanging goals for the session with the person next to them, they'll remain active participants and will be more likely to learn.

Dispel Myths: If the topic covered in the session is at risk of being met with resistance by the audience, address the resistance and set expectations regarding being open-minded during the rest of the session.

Use Break-Outs: People learn best when they are able to work on things and come to their own conclusions. Minimize *telling* and focus on letting them *do something*.

Have a Next Step: Everyone leaving a session should have a next step, and should be held accountable for completing it.

Keep Sessions Tight: It is better to have multiple "modules" than to attempt to expedite by overloading sessions.

Following the guidelines in this section will take instructor-led sessions for new hires from check-the-box onboarding meetings to impactful periods of time where folks learn critical knowledge that will soon be applied. Or, if the criteria we introduced aren't met, maybe some sessions are canceled so that new employees can focus on what they really need to know.

Simulations: Selling

There are several software products that allow salespeople to practice real-world situations without risking a poor performance in front of prospects, and without eating into the bandwidth of other salespeople and management.

Set up simulations that allow salespeople to say the types of things they will say in selling conversations, but without potential negative implications to the business. Simulations are useful for a variety of situations, including:

Opening Meetings: Have salespeople demonstrate the ability to confirm logistics, set a mutual agenda, and discuss what the possible outcomes of the meeting might be.

Telling Stories: Confirm that new hires can tell compelling customer stories.

Off-Script Demo: Observe how the salesperson responds when asked a question about how a certain aspect of their product works that's not part of a standard demo.

Manage Resistance: Hear what the salesperson says when they run into a prospect's objection.

Be creative and leverage simulations to build muscles that will be used when working with real prospects. One point of caution: avoid asking salespeople to perform long-winded monologues, as selling conversations should involve a lot of back-and-forth and not multi-minute speeches by the seller.

Simulations: Prospect Pain

One of the best simulations we run with new hires involves putting salespeople in a prospect's shoes by allowing them to experience the pain that a company's prospects are experiencing, and then observe how it is solved by the solution they sell. This exercise creates buy-in, enthusiasm, and empathy.

Salespeople who have not personally experienced prospect pain are at a disadvantage, as it's challenging to have empathy when talking about a foreign concept. Additionally, salespeople who don't actually understand what's going on in a prospect's world often fail to credibly uncover pain, as a lot of the questions they ask and statements they make show the prospect that the seller has incomplete knowledge of their day-to-day life.

For example, imagine a company that sells software to streamline expense reports. An engaging activity for new hires could be designed as follows:

> *During their first day, a new hire sits down at a desk and is given thirty receipts, all with random notes on them. They are also given a spreadsheet with column headings and one row of sample data. They are asked to input the expenses into the sheet, categorize them based on the type of expense, and add any notes.*
>
> *Once the information is entered, any receipt over $75 must be scanned. All scanned images must be combined into a single file, and submitted, along with the receipt, to the manager via email.*

At this point, the new hire is feeling the pain. To extend this example, consider having them play the role of the manager, as various expenses are accepted and rejected, and then approval is sent along to accounting for payment.

Once the activity is over, have the new hire conduct the same exact tasks in your software, so they can understand the difference between the prospect's current state and their potential future state, should they choose to do business with your company.

Put Down the Firehose

It's tempting to throw a bunch of knowledge at people in their first week. We often hear management make reference to a new hire "drinking from the firehose." Have you ever tried drinking from a firehose? Chances are you'd be wounded and still thirsty. That's exactly what will happen to your new hire, as they will:

- Get discouraged
- Forget it
- By definition, waste their time. Learning something you can't immediately use is a complete waste of time for ramping salespeople. If they can't apply new knowledge or skills *in their job* within 48 hours, training should be delayed.

Why do organizations take this approach? Simple: It's easy.

It's easy for someone who has worked at a company for a while to overwhelm someone who has worked there for a day.

It's easy to know more than the new person.

It's easy to fill days with discussions of 101-level topics.

You know what's hard? Getting a cohort of new hires to walk through your doors and hit quota in their first two full quarters, and then have the next cohort do the same. That's hard, and it requires much more than firehose-like knowledge transfer. It requires a framework.

A Word on All That Product Training

Product training is often the most destructive thing a company can mandate for a new hire. Think about it . . . if someone is brought into a company and taught all about the product, what do you think they will talk about when they get a meeting with a prospect? The product!

In school, students are rewarded for sitting through lectures and then having the ability to regurgitate what they learned on an exam. The more accurate and in-depth their understanding of the material, the better grade they receive. The problem is that organizations take these same individuals, sit them in product training classes, and then expect them to *not* talk about features and benefits, and instead ask pain-based discovery questions. Well, that's counter to everything the person has done in their life, and habits are hard to break.

Yes, salespeople need to understand their product. However, the focus should be on understanding the specific problem that is solved, and that should be the core of the discussion. Excerpt 10.3 demonstrates how to take the features and benefits of a product or service and translate them into the problems that a prospect would need to have to care. These problem statements are the foundation of pain-based discovery questions that salespeople can use to identify winning deals.

Excerpt 10.3: The pain finder

The key to constructing a pain-based discovery question is to understand how a product's features and benefits relate to problems a prospect would have to have to care.

During any product training, we recommend that the matrix below is leveraged to figure out:

1. *For each feature, what are the benefits a prospect would receive?*
2. *For each benefit, what problem would a prospect have to have today to care about the benefit?*

Feature	Benefit	What Problem?

Now, salespeople have identified specific problems that their specific features solve for prospects, and these can be used when asking pain-based discovery questions.

Fortify the Engagement Phase

Use every engagement session as an opportunity to strengthen the content being used for future hires. Specific changes that might be required include:

- **Order**: Change the order of when different concepts are introduced
- **Depth**: Either increase or decrease the depth in which topics are covered
- **Reinforcement**: If critical concepts are not retained by new hires, an opportunity for more robust reinforcement might be required
- **Context**: Abstract concepts are difficult for some people to understand. For example, instead of giving people a written case study about a customer, let them actually meet a customer, hear their story, and have the ability to ask questions.

If known deficiencies exist in the engagement phase, identify opportunities for improvement and execute. There are two common strategies here:

Option 1: Build out the improvements prior to the next cohort starting, without involving the existing cohort of new hires

Option 2: Work with the existing cohort, using their bandwidth and brainpower to build something to be used by future hires

For example, imagine that the new cohort needs to learn about pain experienced by prospects in the oil and gas industry, but there is no existing documentation. One of the most impactful engagement tactics in this situation is to leverage option 2, whereby a subject matter expert on prospect pain in oil and gas (maybe a senior salesperson) gives a speech, and the existing cohort takes what they heard and builds content in the sales playbook. The act of converting what they heard in the session into content for future hires reinforces the knowledge and improves the organization's ability to train new salespeople.

Additionally, one of the jobs of the new hire is to constantly point out what is not clear, what is missing, and what could have been explained better. The trick is to ensure that the people who are responsible for engagement accept this criticism as an attempt to improve the business, and don't view the feedback as personal attacks.

Shadowing Coworkers

A common onboarding tactic is for new hires to "shadow" existing employees. Shadowing includes sitting in on meetings and observing the work of fellow coworkers. Most companies that incorporate shadowing for new employees do it not because it's effective, but because it's easy.

> *"Tim, over the course of your first three days, you'll shadow Suzanne. Let's re-connect Thursday to talk about what you've learned."*

By Thursday, Tim has either obtained a ton of unstructured information that he's trying to make sense of, or he has observed Suzanne's bad habits and he's already headed down the wrong path. Shadowing can have a positive impact, but it must be structured well for engagement. For example:

> *"Tim, I would like you to shadow Suzanne during her discovery calls for the next three days. I want you to pay particular attention to how she plans her day, opens her meetings, asks discovery questions to uncover pain, and the framework she uses to create urgency for the following meeting."*

Tim now has a clear purpose, will be held accountable, and will engage with the shadowing program. Additionally, Suzanne is motivated to execute well, and provide insight on each of these frameworks since she knows that she's setting an example for Tim which will be presented to her manager. Now everyone is engaged. No one is just "onboard" for the ride.

Chapter Summary

- Ensure that all content used relates to specific competencies that new hires must build, and that content is continuously improved and updated.
- Audit instructor-led sessions against the checklist presented in figure 10.2.
- Simulations allow new hires to get confidence-building repetitions before facing high-value prospects.
- Many organizations have new hires "drink from the firehose" because they lack preparation. Avoid this temptation and make the engagement phase as simple as possible, but not simpler.
- Leverage product training only to the extent that it teaches new hires what specific problems the product solves for prospects.
- If new hires are asked to shadow coworkers, ensure that there are clear guidelines for the activity, and that there is mutual accountability to report back what was learned and accomplished.

SECTION 3

Accelerate

TALENT ➡ **ENGAGE** ➡ **ACCELERATE** ➡ **MASTERY**

11

WHAT IS ACCELERATION?

Many organizations plan for the concept of "ramp," which implies that a new hire is climbing toward a fixed destination. That destination is typically considered quota.

Then, the effort and energy put into the new hire's growth diminish, and the sales rep enters the world of performance evaluation solely by revenue attainment. This lack of professional development does a disservice to the employee and to the organization, as continued growth benefits everyone. The best companies continuously accelerate employee development so that an individual continues to develop toward mastery over time.

Sticking with the NFL analogy, can you imagine recruiting a quarterback out of college, getting him to the point of understanding the offense, and then asking him to fend for himself throughout the rest of the season? That would not make for a winning program.

Acceleration starts with the new hire's first meaningful prospect-facing activity, and continues through closing their first full-cycle deal. Following this period, they begin to demonstrate mastery (Section 4), then move into their next role in the organization, at which point the engagement phase begins all over again.

Figure 11.1: The competency rubric for the acceleration phase

Competency	Unsatisfactory	Satisfactory	Excellent

Acceleration should be viewed as the period of time during which a new hire develops the skills required to achieve their goals, and demonstrates strong preliminary success. Figure 11.1 outlines how these competencies can be communicated to the salesperson, along with examples of different levels of performance. Organizations that view "ramp" a period of time will graduate mediocre reps who are ill-equipped to achieve success and deliver erratic results.

Instead, it's key to continuously push the salesperson to the next level. For example, imagine that Kim, a newly hired account executive, just completed a demo certification. In lieu of celebrating and never working with Kim again on demos, an organization truly committed to accelerating her performance would, in turn, focus on the following advanced demo scenarios:

- Different personas
- Various personas in one room
- A prospect who has stated they prefer another vendor for specific reasons
- A combination of some people live and some people remote, a tricky logistical challenge

The scenarios above demonstrate that just because someone did the basics well, there's no guarantee that they're ready for these more challenging real-life scenarios that will inevitably arise.

An outcomes-based acceleration phase helps set clear expectations with a salesperson, where they know exactly what they need to accomplish and how to get there. Time-based ramp, on the other hand, creates mutual frustration between the employee and management. A struggling employee in the latter scenario believes that the required time to ramp has passed, while management might believe that performance was not met.

Chapter Summary

- The acceleration phase ensures that the developing skills necessary for the new hire to achieve long-term success are supported by the organization.
- Acceleration must go beyond the basics and address the different scenarios that the salesperson will run into when working deals.

12

FIRST ACTIVITY TO FIRST DEAL

Once a salesperson has begun to perform activities, the next major milestone is to close their first deal. There's a catch though. We're talking about the first deal that they worked from beginning to end, within their target market, using the same resources that they will use while working future deals. There are several types of "first deals" that shouldn't count, including:

One-Off: Closing a customer with a rare or one-of-a-kind use case that is not representative of future deals

Hero-Assisted: Any deal where the manager played a key role in the later stages, while the rep sat and watched

Tee Ball: Deals that were assigned to the rep mid-sales cycle and were already on their way to closing

Layup: Extraordinarily "easy" deals, where the customer bought without going through all of the stages of the sales process, or without including other stakeholders that would be customary in almost any opportunity

The point of measuring the first deal is simply to confirm that the rep is able to see results from all of the engagement work that has been put in to date, at which point the focus shifts toward acceleration and achieving quota over the course of consecutive quarters.

On the way to their first deal, there are several intermediate milestones that should be tracked, including:

- First activity at each stage of the sales process
- Learning and certifying on the key activities they will complete over the course of a sales process
- Lost deals, including the reason lost and analysis of whether anything could have been done differently

Now that the new hires have been through the engagement phase, the acceleration phase is where coaching starts to happen, and it should happen frequently. If your sales managers are not certified coaches, we have incorporated an introduction to the C.O.A.C.H. framework from our book *Coaching Salespeople* in excerpt 12.1.

Excerpt 12.1: The C.O.A.C.H. framework

The C.O.A.C.H. framework allows managers to consistently and effectively close the gap between individual performance-to-competence and create ongoing accountability. Here is the framework:

Challenge: *Identify the challenges the salesperson faces, and then only pick the one that most readily accessible with the highest potential impact. Identify if it is a mind-set, activity, or skillset challenge.*

Outline: *The manager must outline the potential paths to growth prior to meeting with the salesperson.* **Action**: *During the actual coaching conversation, the manager and salesperson must co-create an action plan that is within the salesperson's control. Strong coaches uncover this plan by asking questions.*

Consequences: *Ensure that the salesperson understands the consequences of failing to execute the co-created action plan. These need not be draconian, but effective coaching ensures that there is no mystification around expectations. There are three types of consequences: personal, professional, and organizational.*

> **Hold Accountable**: *Outline clear next steps that both the salesperson and manager can be held accountable to, and set a time to review progress.*
>
> *Employing this framework ensures highly-impactful, low-friction, consistent coaching conversations. Applying this framework is the single most effective means of accelerating salesperson growth.*

A low-friction and highly-effective way to coach salespeople is to listen to their calls. Several software vendors offer products that take recorded calls and allow managers to analyze them in a variety of ways, including by listening to specific sections of a call or by observing metadata, such as talk time and how frequently the salesperson and prospect took turns speaking. Creating call coaching rubrics will allow for consistent coaching of calls and will also ensure that salespeople know the key elements they are being judged on as they speak with prospects.

Chapter Summary

- Defining the acceleration phase as the first meaningful activity (such as a discovery call with a prospect in the salesperson's target market) to a won deal maintains focus and momentum.
- To exit the acceleration phase, the first deal must be representative of the types of deals the salesperson will be closing in the long term, the new hire must run the full sales cycle, and management shouldn't assist with a hero-close.
- Coaching must happen frequently during the acceleration phase to course-correct on any deficiencies that management observes and set the salesperson up for long-term success.

13

CERTIFICATIONS

A comprehensive certification program drives salespeople to accelerate their performance and achieve their goals. Lawyers graduate from law school and pass the arduous bar exam. Accountants get master's degrees and then pass the CPA exam. Doctors go through medical school, residency, fellowship, and pass countless exams along the way. Salespeople, on the other hand, often have an education unrelated to sales, go through a two-week onboarding program, and are told to hit their quota. That's unprofessional.

High-performers who want to be professionals embrace certification programs. They view certifications as an opportunity to stress-test their current skillset and to learn something new. It's critical for *team* success that employees know that everyone else on the team has demonstrated the same degree of rigor, weeding out the mediocrity that sucks the energy out of an organization.

We are not suggesting that you drop recent hires into a classroom and keep them there until they have passed a bunch of certification exams. Certification must be tied to acquired and developing skills relevant to the near-term job-to-be done. Each skill they need to demonstrate should be laid out in a format similar to that in figure 13.1.

Figure 13.1: Certification depth

Skill	Know It	Do It	Do It Well	Do It Well Under Pressure
Ask pain-based discovery questions				
Run an entire discovery call				
Show a compelling product demo				
Convert trade show conversations into sales opportunities				
Manage resistance related to the competition				

Certifications must exist in one of two formats:

Basic certifications center around the person's knowledge and their ability to execute at a basic level. The goal is to get them proficient enough to start conducting an activity. These happen in a controlled setting and do not account for the individual's application of concepts learned in the real world.

Advanced certifications provide greater depth and look at the extent to which someone can apply what they have learned. Here, edge cases that are beyond the scope of the basic certification are introduced. To receive advanced certifications, individuals must not only excel in the classroom, but must also achieve real-world milestones.

The key difference between the two is that the advance certification stress-tests the person's ability to get results from the knowledge they have acquired. Demo certifications are a great example. Basic certifications might require the following:

- *Demo the product based on a mock discovery call*
- *Apply all relevant sales methodology frameworks throughout the demo*
- *Set clear next steps and get the prospect's agreement*

While an advanced demo certification would go a step further:

- *Consistently demonstrate all basic certification traits on live demos*
- *Achieve a demo-to-close rate of at least 30%*
- *Achieve quota in at least two consecutive quarters*

The bottom line for certifications is as follows:

If salespeople can't do something in a controlled practice situation, they will not be able to do it under pressure with a prospect.

The Forgetting Curve

If you were presented with an algebra problem right now, how confident are you that you could solve it? What about the kingdom, phylum, class, and order of humans? The difference between Corinthian, Ionic, and Doric columns? You may have spent hundreds of hours of your life learning these subjects, but if you're like most people, you don't remember much, since the opportunity to apply them in sales is rare.

In school, we did worksheets, took quizzes, and endured tests—all so we could prepare for the dreaded final exam. Why did our teachers put us through this battery of exercises instead of just telling us what to remember and have us take a test? The answer lies in the fact that the human mind is terrible at remembering things that we have only been exposed to a limited number of times.

Certification helps reinforce what has previously been learned and ensures that a sufficient level of knowledge and skill is retained, so it can be put to use. As soon as humans learn something new, they begin to lose that knowledge, as demonstrated by the *forgetting curve* in figure 13.2.

Figure 13.2: The forgetting curve

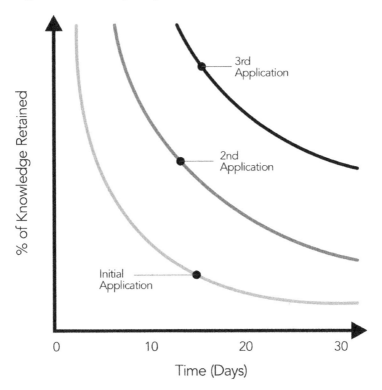

In the late 1800s, German psychologist Hermann Ebbinghaus performed research that resulted in the concept of the forgetting curve. He found that after thirty-one days, only 21% of knowledge is retained unless it is revisited. The more it's revisited, the stronger the retention. The fascinating part about the slope of the curve is that it's so steep immediately after information is learned, that only 33% of knowledge is retained after one day without a reminder. It's also interesting that humans have not changed learning capability in 200 years in spite of the volume of information and technological innovation.

Regardless of how smart someone is or how much experience they have, if you stick them in a "drink from the firehose" boot camp, they will not remember hardly anything unless it's continuously revisited.

A Note on Adult Learning

In the following sections, we introduce a winning formula to roll out certifications in a way that ensures salespeople can skillfully execute the activities critical for success in their job. Along the path to success, there is a lot of hard work, learning, and failure that new hires will need to endure prior to coming out of the other side as a quota-achieving hero.

Our process of developing certification programs is built upon a strong foundation of adult learning and instructional design skills and experience. However, we will not go deep into these concepts in this book, as a worthwhile explanation would fill an excessive number of pages, and great books have already been written on these topics.

For further reading, we suggest the following books:

- *Make It Stick*
- *The ABCs of How We Learn*
- *Design for How People Learn*

Multiple-Choice Quizzes

The most basic way we test sales knowledge is through the multiple-choice quiz. Here, new hires will confirm that they can recognize information when presented with a question and a set of choices.

Multiple-choice, however, is not enough. Quizzes alone do not make for valid certification criteria. Knowledge and recognition skills are not enough to do the job effectively, but do provide a great foundation for launching into the more robust aspects of a certification program.

Use multiple-choice quizzes to ensure basic knowledge retention and to identify deficiencies that must be addressed. However, do not think that just because someone passes a multiple-choice test that they are prepared to hit their quota.

Scenarios

Introducing real-world scenarios that make people think hard is a key part of a world-class certification program. In school, we were often required to show our work to demonstrate that we not only knew the right answer, but that we also knew *how to get to the right answer.* There's a reason that this process was required in school: if you can't show your work, then you don't actually understand the application of the concept.

Beyond multiple-choice quizzes, scenarios challenge salespeople to demonstrate an understanding of the concepts critical to their role. Here are a few ways to present challenges:

Simple Scenario: A one–two sentence question that requires an open-ended response. An example: *"A prospect was supposed to bring his boss to a demo, and the boss didn't show up. What do you do?"* Scenarios might also include a content asset, such as a screenshot of the CRM, to add additional context.

Written Vignette: A one–two page scenario that outlines something relevant to the salesperson's role that they will need to solve using frameworks. Following the vignette, including multiple-choice questions, open-ended questions, and activities to stress-test the salesperson's application of frameworks.

Call Recording with Prompt: Play a portion of a sales call and ask a question that challenges the salesperson to apply frameworks they have learned. This method of delivery is especially impactful, because it mirrors the interaction a salesperson will have on the job.

The key difference between the scenario challenge and the multiple-choice test is that the salesperson does not know specifically which framework(s) to apply or how, so they require more critical thinking than picking an answer to a multiple-choice question.

Scenarios can be developed and presented live, using word processing documents or an online learning platform that allows salespeople to respond and have their peers or managers offer feedback. Purchasing a tool before understanding your goals and certification process is not advised.

We have included an example of a few scenarios at HireOnboardRamp.com.

Case Studies

Critical thinking is one of the most important skills for salespeople to establish and practice, and doing so in a controlled environment is a great way to truly assess their abilities without the random influences of the outside world that salespeople constantly face.

Business schools around the world use case studies as learning tools that present students with a complex set of information, then ask them to conduct analysis and make recommendations based on what they have read. Using case studies is a great way to accelerate the success of a recently hired salesperson.

A case study for an account executive might start with a current view of their sales pipeline, with vital deal details (close dates, deal sizes, etc.), discovery notes, and information about next steps. The case can then introduce additional exhibits such as snippets from calls, email threads with prospects, and conversations with the salesperson's manager.

At the end of the case, the salesperson is asked to make a decision on one or more topics, and provide their rationale for doing so in their response.

Unlike multiple-choice questions, where it's often easy to eliminate a couple of bad choices and take a swing, salespeople must truly understand the material in order to succeed in a case study. The case study is a step beyond scenarios as well, as they will include many different variables that need to be analyzed simultaneously.

Those who succeed in these simulated examples have had their relevant critical thinking skills stress-tested to ensure they are in a position to succeed. Those who fail have failed in a specific way, and management can then focus on coaching or training their developing skills and making improvements. Or, management finds out early that the salesperson isn't going to make it.

Case studies can take many forms. We have included a simple example at HireOnboardRamp.com.

Observation of Real-World Activities

Incorporating real-life performance into a certification program greatly increases the value and relevance of the achievement. For example, a demo certification should include each of the elements outlined in this chapter, and should also involve a review of real-life demos provided to prospects. It is smart to require a certain number of demos to convert to won business as well, as an academic-only certification falls short of having an impact on the organization.

The more quantitative observed performance can be, the better. For example, if the focus is on discovery certification, metrics to track are conversion rates from the discovery stage of the sales process to the next stage (such as demo). Another metric to examine is how many days prospects stay in the discovery stage, since shorter stage duration indicates that salespeople are able to uncover pain to move to the next stage, or disqualify quickly.

Make performance observations quantitative creating a scoring rubric, such as the demo certification rubric shown in figure 13.3.

Figure 13.3: A simplified discovery certification rubric

Category	Did not (0)	Did it (1)	Did it well (2)
Maintained Rapport			
Uncovered Pain			
Discussed High-Level Pricing			
Managed Resistance			
Has Clear Next Steps			

What we see in figure 13.3 is similar to how medical students and residents are graded when learning to perform procedures on patients. By providing a scoring rubric and a definition of what it means to score at each level over a variety of categories, it's possible to turn what would otherwise be a qualitative exercise into a well-defined quantitative feedback loop to help assess the current state of performance and drive continuous improvement.

Eliminating Certification Anxiety

By creating an immersive environment for certification, an organization can avoid skewing toward people who are good or bad at taking tests. Instead, the core focus becomes achieving practical mastery, which is what matters most. Practical mastery is a journey, unlike a "test-taking event." This structure significantly reduces anxiety and creates a fair and impactful way to grow teams consistently.

By clarifying expectations around the fact that certification is a learning opportunity and not a punitive program, and by reinforcing the belief that learning is a process, not an event, the stakes are reduced and performance dramatically improves in certification activities. We recommend giving employees ample practice quizzes that are solely theirs to practice, prior to a formal certification exam. This way, they are given a fair chance to learn the material, practice recall, revisit gaps, and eventually perform well on certification test-outs.

What If People Fail?

Salespeople are going to fail. Period. That's fantastic! It builds resilience and an appetite for continued development when a salesperson realizes that the world did not end. The responsibility of management is to ensure that failure occurs in a controlled internal learning environment (which can include actual selling conversations).

The worst thing a manager can do for an employee is to put them in a job in which they are not positioned for success. When a salesperson fails a certification, management has one simple question to ask:

> *Based on the current state and future potential of the individual, does it make sense to invest the required energy necessary to get them to where they need to be?*

If so, execute! If not, then initiate a plan to manage them out of the role (or company), and revisit what went wrong in the talent identification process to get them to where they are today.

Chapter Summary

- Certifications are the single best tool that management can apply to ensure that salespeople are successful.
- The Ebbinghaus forgetting curve dictates that 79% of knowledge is lost after thirty-one days if it's not revisited. Furthermore, 67% of knowledge is lost after just one day without a reminder.
- Multiple-choice quizzes, scenarios, case studies, and the observation of real-world activity are key components of a strong certification program.

SECTION 4

Mastery

TALENT ➡ **ENGAGE** ➡ **ACCELERATE** ➡ **MASTERY**

14

FIRST DEAL TO REPEAT QUOTA ATTAINMENT

When a salesperson closes their first full-cycle deal, that's simply one small step toward achieving mastery in their role. Similar to setting strict guidelines for the definition of "first deal," the mastery phase exists to ensure that attaining quota is a prescriptive and repeatable process. The goal is not to constantly spin plates with reps hitting and missing goals. The goal is to create consistent on-target performance.

Along this path, it's critical to have formal health checks at specific milestones to ensure that the trajectory that the salesperson is following is directly leading to mastery. Pipeline coverage and quota attainment milestones are two key metrics discussed in this chapter.

Full Pipeline Coverage

An early milestone on the path to mastery is full pipeline coverage, meaning that if they close every deal in their pipeline, they will achieve their quota.

Here is a checklist to inspect pipeline coverage:

- ☐ All opportunities fall within the salesperson's target market
- ☐ Exit criteria have been satisfied for each opportunity prior to moving it to the next stage
- ☐ X% of opportunities have a next step that the prospect has agreed to, and a meeting is on the calendar

This simple checklist will indicate if the salesperson is applying what was covered during the engagement and acceleration phases. If there are issues, they are quickly identified and addressed while minimal time is lost. Yes, there are more metrics that we will introduce later on to gauge salesperson performance, but it's important to focus on the most critical data points and ensure they are nailed down before going overboard on accountability frameworks. As we discussed extensively in *Coaching Salespeople*:

> *Coaching one item results in focus and results. Coaching several items creates a lack of focus and often ends in a step backward.*

Start with pipeline coverage because if a salesperson doesn't have deals in their pipeline, it's impossible to hit quota.

Figure 14.1 shows an example of a salesperson who has achieved full pipeline coverage when their quota is $150,000 and the total value of their pipeline closing this quarter is also $150,000.

Figure 14.1: Full pipeline coverage for someone with a $150k per quarter quota

Stage	Total Value
1 - Discovery	100,000
2 - Demo	30,000
3 - Proposal	10,000
4 - Closing	10,000
Total	150,000

Full Quota Coverage

After full pipeline coverage, the next milestone is full quota coverage, where the expected value of their pipeline equals their quota. Each stage of the sales process should have a projected close rate associated with it to calculate the expected value of the pipeline. These close rates should be monitored on a quarterly or annual basis, and adjusted based on real data. If you do not have accurate close rates associated with each stage, see excerpt 14.2 from our book *Financial Modeling for Startups*.

Excerpt 14.2: Calculating pipeline expected value

The total value of a sales pipeline can be mislead-
ing, as it does not indicate how likely that pipeline is
to close. As a result, *expected pipeline value* is a better
metric, as shown in the table below.

Stage	Total Value	Win %	Expected Value
1 - Discovery	400,000	10%	40,000
2 - Demo	250,000	30%	75,000
3 - Proposal	100,000	60%	60,000
4 - Closing	50,000	90%	45,000
Total	800,000		220,000

In the table above, we simply take the total value
at each stage, multiply this number by that stage's
win %, and that calculation results in the expected
value. The sum of the expected value column then
equals the total expected value of the pipeline.

This calculation is useful at the company-level to
help with high-level forecasting, but drill-down is
required to actually drive decision making. Looking
at the individual team and rep level will help managers identify opportunities to do more of what is
working, or can help them find pipeline issues that
can be coached.

Once the total expected value in the table in excerpt 14.2 equals or exceeds the salesperson's quota, they have achieved full quota coverage.

The checklist for full quota coverage must include the following:

☐ All opportunities fall within the salesperson's target market

☐ Exit criteria have been satisfied for each opportunity prior to moving it to the next stage

☐ X% of opportunities have a next step that the prospect has agreed to on the calendar

☐ Projected deal sizes are realistic

☐ Close dates are real based on the prospect's timeline

This checklist introduces two new items that are very important to monitor as salespeople develop mastery. The first looks at projected deal sizes. The goal here is to ensure that the salesperson is thinking critically about the actual opportunity, and not just putting placeholder numbers that may or may not be real. Depending on your business, placeholders might make sense in the very early stages of the sales cycle, but they should be adjusted as more is known about the deal, especially as the probability to close increases and each dollar of projected value has a reciprocal impact on expected pipeline value.

Additionally, close rates should be real based on buyer timeline. If a salesperson's pipeline looks like figure 14.3, there's a problem.

Figure 14.3: End-of-quarter close dates are not realistic

Opportunity Name	Close Date
Alpha Corp	3/31
Beta Co.	3/31
Charlie Inc.	3/31
Delta LLC	6/30

A pipeline full of close dates that are on the last day of the quarter indicates that the salesperson doesn't have clarity around when deals are closing, but has high hopes that they are going to close in-quarter.

25% Quota Attainment

At the point where the salesperson has achieved 25% of their quota, they have demonstrated that they can close some deals, or at least that they can close one large deal. Our checklist at 25% quota attainment includes:

- ☐ All opportunities fall within the salesperson's target market
- ☐ Exit criteria have been satisfied for each opportunity prior to moving it to the next stage
- ☐ X% of opportunities have a next step that the prospect has agreed to on the calendar

☐ Projected deal sizes are realistic

☐ Close dates are real based on the prospect's timeline

☐ All lost deals have an associated reason, and coaching has occurred around any deals that should not have been lost

The new addition to this checklist examines lost deals. Here, we are ensuring that two points are present:

- Salespeople are losing for reasons that fall into the losing zone
- They actually understand why they are losing

Excerpt 14.4 reviews the concept of the winning zone from *Triangle Selling*, a key concept that salespeople must understand to focus their energy on deals they will win, and disqualify losers fast.

Excerpt 14.4: The winning zone

> Every product has a losing zone, a battlefield, and a winning zone. The losing zone consists of the features, benefits, and problems solved that a salesperson's product or service simply cannot effectively compete with in a competitive deal. The battlefield is that area of parity where there might be different approaches but similar results can be realized, regardless of which vendor a prospect selects. Salespeople should focus the bulk of their energy

on the winning zone. This area represents the set of problems a salesperson's product or service solves more effectively than the competition (keeping in mind that the competition might include "do-it-yourself").

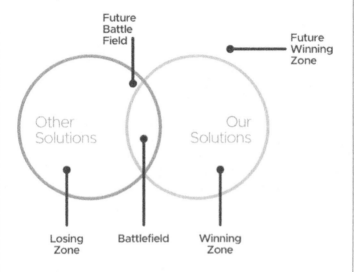

Asking prospects questions that uncover pain in the winning zone might lead to early disqualification, which is why few salespeople focus here. We suggest that salespeople should focus on fewer conversations with a higher likelihood of winning business, instead of a high volume with prospects that will never buy, or worse—perceive the salesperson's product as a commodity, leaving them to compete solely upon price.

50% Quota Attainment

At 50% of quota, some degree of repeatability has been observed.

- ☐ All opportunities fall within the salesperson's target market
- ☐ Exit criteria have been satisfied for each opportunity prior to moving it to the next stage
- ☐ X% of opportunities have a next step that the prospect has agreed to on the calendar
- ☐ Projected deal sizes are realistic
- ☐ Close dates are real based on the prospect's timeline
- ☐ All lost deals have an associated reason, and coaching has occurred around any deals that should not have been lost
- ☐ The length of the sales cycle for each won deal is in-line with expectations

Now we have added a metric to gauge the length of the sales cycle. If the salesperson is taking longer than expected to close deals, management must identify possible coaching opportunities.

80% Quota Attainment

The salesperson is getting close! Here's what the revised checklist looks like.

- ☐ All opportunities fall within the salesperson's target market

- ☐ Exit criteria have been satisfied for each opportunity prior to moving it to the next stage
- ☐ X% of opportunities have a next step that the prospect has agreed to on the calendar
- ☐ Projected deal sizes are realistic
- ☐ Close dates are real based on the prospect's timeline
- ☐ All lost deals have an associated reason, and coaching has occurred around any deals that should not have been lost
- ☐ The length of the sales cycle for each won deal is in line with expectations
- ☐ Win rates are in line with expectations

At this point, there is a significant amount of data, so it's time to look at win rates and compare them against what was expected. Salespeople with lower win rates than expected are either leaving money on the table by losing deals they should win, or are focusing energy on deals outside of their winning zone.

Full Quota Attainment

Now we're cooking with gas! The salesperson has achieved quota, and is on the path to fitting in with the team.

- ☐ All opportunities fall within the salesperson's target market
- ☐ Exit criteria have been satisfied for each opportunity prior to moving it to the next stage

☐ X% of opportunities have a next step that the prospect has agreed to on the calendar

☐ Projected deal sizes are realistic

☐ Close dates are real based on the prospect's timeline

☐ All lost deals have an associated reason, and coaching has occurred around any deals that should not have been lost

☐ The length of the sales cycle for each won deal is in line with expectations

☐ Win rates are in line with expectations

☐ Time to full quota attainment

The metric added here is time to full quota attainment. If quota was reached in the first or second quarter, that's a good sign. If it took longer than that after repeat misses, then the big question to ask is whether or not the salesperson is at the point where sustained production is worth it for the organization, and if not, if they are at the point where they are willing and able to get to that milestone.

Back-to-Back Quota Attainment

Given enough attempts, anyone can make a three-pointer, bowl a strike, or hit a bullseye on the dartboard. The percentage of people who can do so twice in a row is exponentially lower, and these are the people who have demonstrated mastery of their role. Yes, there is always room to improve, but someone who has attained quota in back-to-back quarters while satisfying each checklist in this chapter is positioned for long-term success in their role.

As a salesperson works to attain quota for the second quarter in a row, continue to monitor the milestones we looked at on their path to hitting quota for the first time. If they are achieving these milestones faster than they did the first time, that's a great sign. If the pace is slowed, look for coaching opportunities and continue to help the salesperson fill in gaps.

Chapter Summary

- Mastery is demonstrated as a result of back-to-back quota attainment.
- Incremental milestones are critical to ensure that a salesperson is on pace to achieve mastery, and management must course-correct if not.
- Key milestones on the path to back-to-back quota attainment include full pipeline coverage, full quota coverage, 25% quota attainment, 50% quota attainment, 80% quota attainment, and 100% quota attainment.

15

F.I.R.E.
UNDERPERFORMERS

Our focus is always on supporting the professional and personal development of individuals through the use of frameworks. Nevertheless, no matter how well the T.E.A.M. framework is implemented, not every new hire will be successful. After failing to meet expectations, some will look for other roles within the company, others will seek employment elsewhere, and the underperformers who fail to improve and don't take the initiative to leave their role on their own will need to be terminated. The F.I.R.E. framework guides managers on how to swiftly and fairly deal with problem employees.

Formalize the Conversation

Once management has identified that an employee is on the path toward termination, the conversation must be formalized. Casual feedback such as "I think you can do better" is insufficient and must be replaced with a formal human resources process and direct language such as "If you are unable to perform the minimum sales activity required, you will be terminated."

Direct and formal language makes it clear to the employee that the tone has shifted, and mitigates the risk that the employee or their coworkers will find subsequent action unfair.

> **Manager:** *You have missed quota the last two quarters because you have not met your activity goals. If you are unable to meet activity goals each month this quarter, you will be terminated.*

Invite Resolution

Once the conversation has been formalized, invite the employee to resolve the problem. This process accomplishes a few things:

- It gets the employee to recognize that there is a specific problem
- The problem becomes well-defined
- A path to resolution is outlined and agreed upon
- Since the employee is involved in the development of the resolution, they now have buy-in and ownership

> **Manager:** *Given what we've discussed, what measurable activity can you do from here to get back on track?*

> **Salesperson**: *I need to source ten new targeted leads per day, ensure that I make all of my cold calls, and confirm that each email sequence is being delivered. My commitment is to spend an hour block each morning and afternoon prospecting, and also plan for each sales meeting at least one day in advance. I believe that these activities combined will allow me to achieve my goal.*

Giving employees ownership of the resolution is key, as managers too often spend tremendous amounts of energy trying to fix something that the employee doesn't even know is a problem.

If the proposed resolution is not sufficient, the manager can always adjust course by recommending alternatives.

Realign Expectations

Create immediate, and short-term milestones to help the employee address the problem. Document these expectations in a performance improvement plan (PIP) that details the salesperson's activity commitments, the expected outcomes of these activities, the frequency of check-ins with management, and the date on which performance will be evaluated.

> **Manager**: *I will document what we covered here today in a performance improvement plan that I will email to you by the end of the day. We will meet weekly throughout the quarter and will have a final meeting the day after this quarter*

ends to review your results and determine the future of your employment with our company.

The only things a salesperson can control are the quality and quantity of activity, so simply stating outcomes is not sufficient. In order to exit the PIP, they must perform the agreed-upon activity *and* achieve the desired results.

Execute the Decision

When the evaluation date arrives, management must execute the decision by taking one of the following actions:

- Continue to employ the salesperson without the PIP in place
- Extend the PIP
- Terminate employment

If the salesperson met the goals outlined in the PIP and appears to be a promising long-term asset for the company, that's great news! If they were close, management might extend the PIP and continue to closely monitor performance. However, if the salesperson did not achieve their goal, it's time to terminate employment or find them a new role within the organization.

By following the F.I.R.E. framework, the negative impact on culture as a result of the termination will be minimal. Remaining employees will see that the fired salesperson was given a fair chance to meet expectations and failed. While firing might rattle the team in some organizations, it is far worse to keep people around who constantly underperform.

Chapter Summary

- Use the F.I.R.E. framework to help struggling employees improve performance, and if they can't, manage them out of their role.

16

KEYS TO T.E.A.M. FRAMEWORK SUCCESS

Congratulations! You now have the framework to build and grow your sales team using the T.E.A.M. framework:

Talent Acquisition: Identify, interview, and hire the right people, at the right time, to achieve business goals

Engage New Hires: Convert candidates to producers, quickly getting them up to speed and executing revenue-producing activities

Accelerate Performance: Drive continuous improvement around competencies that lead to consistent results

Mastery and Progression: Achieve mastery in the current role, and develop both strategic and tactical competencies for future positions within the organization

It's critical that no one person shoulders the burden of building a world-class sales team. Think about how to assign roles to different folks in your organization based on their expertise.

Build out job aids for the team. These assets can be electronic or physical documents (it's amazing how much people love two-sided laminates) and act as quick-reference guides. Putting your sales methodology on a front-and-back laminate that a salesperson carries around with them increases the probability that they'll use it and not revert to something that's easier and not effective. Examples of job aids that we have seen be effective include:

Discovery Guide: A document that guides sellers on how to prepare for, navigate, and follow up on discovery conversations

Demo Flow: Core guidelines on what an effective demo entails, as well as common variations

Persona and Use Case Guides: Advanced guidance on how a product or service applies to specific personas and/or use cases

Methodology Overview: A laminate with all of the key elements of the sales methodology for quick reference

The information described here will also be in the sales playbook, but when someone is struggling with a specific topic, such as executing discovery meetings, a concise overview of effective discovery printed out on their desk and referenced constantly will help improve performance.

It's a T.E.A.M. Effort

When implementing the strategies outlined in this book, here are some groups of people who need to step into key roles:

High-Potential Individual Contributors: Since they're on the front lines on a day-to-day basis, they will provide a lot of the raw and uncut material that will be key to developing a strong program.

Sales Managers: Identify specific challenges and areas for improvement within their existing team.

Customer Success: These are the people who have to "clean up after" underperforming salespeople when they oversell deals. Customer Success Managers (CSMs) are a great source of insight into how to improve sales performance.

Marketing: Like CSMs, folks on the marketing team sees the performance of individual salespeople through a peer or teammate lens, and often have insights that they can share to inform stronger new hire development.

Sales Leadership: Work with finance, HR, and other key stakeholders to ensure that the organization is equipped to attract the right people, make them productive, and keep them around as they continue to grow in their careers.

Keep your program simple. Resist the temptation to "do more stuff." The temptation to address every edge case and go deeper on topics than is needed is real. Additionally, some employees tend to think that "more is better," when, in fact, the reality is typically that "less is more." Attention should be given to removing complexity, not adding it.

Whatever you do, don't take your eye off of the continuous improvement of the application of the T.E.A.M. framework. Each individual and cohort entering the organization should be better positioned for success than the last, and future roles should increasingly be filled with internal candidates who are being groomed for promotions within or across departments.

AFTERWORD

People don't really think about sales being a team sport. I know I didn't. I started my sales career because I wanted to own my destiny, decide when and how much I'd work, and how much I'd make. I thought it was like owning my own business without the hassle.

Over the course of the next twenty-five years, I'd realize that while all sales reps may own a quota, selling was more than just closing deals. Someone really was "running that business" or greasing the wheels, improving my ability to sell. I realized that I got more excited about improving the sales process or helping multiple salespeople sell more than I did just closing my deals. I started focusing on sales operations to build infrastructure that made it easier for reps to close deals, but didn't really get that the sales process was more exciting for me than the sale itself until my first job as VP of Sales.

As the first VP Sales at NetSuite in 1999, I was employee number seven and built a sales team responsible for the first $30m in revenue. With our first per user price set at $4.95 per month, that's a lot of individual sales to enable. Sales enablement or sales productivity was where I belonged.

For the past ten years, I've helped many companies scale their sales teams using process, metrics, and "enablement tools." Companies told me "our sales team *just isn't hitting the number*" or "the revenue isn't predictable" or "our reps don't know to talk about our value proposition or differentiate us." Over time I realized that sales reps weren't really the issue but the "environment" or infrastructure we ask them to work in is what needed improvement! For some, it was creating better sales messaging; for others, it was creating a cohesive sales strategy and process; for many, it was helping with day-to-day sales management execution.

But, true "sales enablement" is more than just fixing problems. It needs to start with the hiring process:

> *How do we work with HR (or external recruiters) to define the job, recruit the right people, assess and interview them effectively, onboard them so they ramp quickly and teach a young management team to coach them in a way that improves retention?*

I recently left consulting to work full time with a former client that was growing exponentially. As Head of Sales Productivity, some of the immediate projects focused not on the sales process, CRM, or other tools and infrastructure, but on hiring and onboarding. We were hiring up to six new reps each month, opening our first remote office (which compounds the problem), and had a fairly young management team. How do we quickly scale a sales team and get them producing quickly? I really needed to assess our current candidate profile, recruiting, and interview process, and then create an onboarding program and teach managers to coach as opposed to diving in and closing the sale.

Without an effective hiring or onboarding program in place, the experience usually resembles the following: We leave the "recruiting" to HR and then complain we don't like the candidates they bring in. I watched as candidates came in and were passed around to five different people (many asked the same questions). The worst part was once hired they were "handed off" to their managers. No wonder every sales rep does their own thing, or it can take ten months to make them productive.

To begin with, we needed to look at the above as a single process rather than disparate events. We started by better defining the type of person we were looking to hire and finding better ways to get referrals for these folks. Next, we looked at our "hiring criteria" and built rubrics based on those criteria.

By getting all the managers on the same page around the recruiting or sourcing and interview process, we were able to implement a sales skills assessment prior to bringing people in for onsite interviews. When bringing people onsite for multiple interviews, we implemented a structured process to have each interviewer focus on different areas.

This made our interview process more engaging for the candidate as well as more informative for us.

Bottom line: We recently made six offers at a two-day staffing event in our second location and had them all start on the same day. We now look at recruiting, interviewing, assessing, and onboarding as part of a process—not unrelated events. We are able learn from each new cohort and improve the process as we help new hires get initially engaged and accelerate them on their path to mastery.

Jodi Maxson

APPENDIX A: OTHER CLOZELOOP BOOKS

If you like what you've read here, check out the other sales books we have written.

Triangle Selling

Fast growth is the name of the game for sales organizations. Long-term success hinges upon a sales team with core skills and tactical frameworks that drive repeatable results.

Regardless of existing sales methodology, market, and company size, *Triangle Selling* empowers salespeople, managers, and executives to quickly adopt the fundamentals necessary to fuel consistent growth within their organization, onboard effectively, and remain agile in an ever-evolving profession.

from the authors of
The Sales Enablement Playbook
and
Sales Development

TRIANGLE SELLING

Sales Fundamentals to Fuel Growth

hilmon sorey   cory bray

Like doctors, lawyers, and engineers who learn fundamental skills and frameworks to drive their work, this third book by industry veterans Sorey and Bray spells out, in practical language, the fundamentals of selling.

The Sales Enablement Playbook
In *The Sales Enablement Playbook*, we provide insights into creating a culture of sales enablement throughout your organization. This book provides a series of stand-alone chapters with frameworks and tactics that you can immediately implement, regardless of company size or industry. Whether you are a sales executive, a sales practitioner, or a non-sales executive looking for ways to impact growth, *The Sales Enablement Playbook* will help you identify your role in a thriving enablement ecosystem.

Sales Development

Sales development is one of the fastest-growing careers in the United States. It is fast-paced, often on the leading edge of technology, and people in the role have the possibility of making a ton of money!

Unlike accounting, medicine, or law, most salespeople do not study their profession in college. Instead, they are tossed into the fray without much training, context, or support and are left to sink or swim. This method proves neither efficient nor effective for the individual or the company.

Sales Development is specifically written for the job seeker or individual contributor who has aspirations of success in a sales development role, and beyond. This is your personal guidebook to the how, why, and what-to-dos of the sales development profession. Written practically and tactically, this book shows you how to get the job, how to perform, and how to position yourself for advancement. Based upon ten years of teaching sales development representatives in the fastest-growing companies in the United States, this book will launch you on your path to becoming a rock star.

from the authors of
The Sales Enablement Playbook.

SALES
DEVELOPMENT

cory bray   hilmon sorey

foreword by chris beall
afterword by ryan reisert

Table of Contents:

Sales Playbooks: The Builder's Toolkit

A well-designed, relevant, and highly utilized sales playbook creates teams that engage with more prospects, produce more pipeline, and close more deals. A playbook creates more consistent top performers, more quickly. It will also close the gap between your top performers and everyone else.

Playbooks are living tools that must continue to be developed, revised, and curated over time. Growing companies are constantly hiring new people, promoting internally, entering into new markets, and facing direct or unforeseen competition. In order to drive success, an understanding of how the business operates, what has worked in the past, what is presently working, and what is anticipated to work in the future is required.

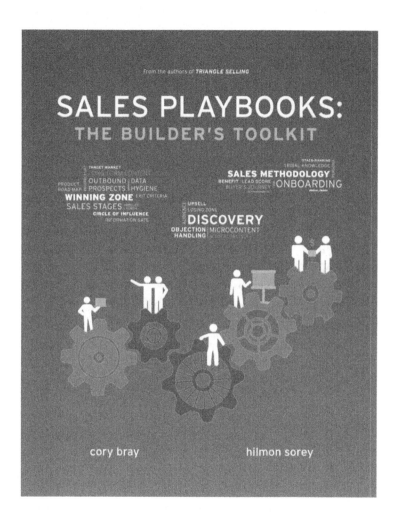

Chapter 1: Introduction
Chapter 2: Gathering Information
Chapter 3: Interviews
Chapter 4: Blueprint Creation

Chapter 5: Discovery Questions
Chapter 6: Personas
Chapter 7: The Sales Process
Chapter 8: Target Market
Chapter 9: Customer Stories
Chapter 10: Managing Resistance (Objections)
Chapter 11: Competitive Battlecards
Chapter 12: Products and Pricing
Chapter 13: Structuring Meetings
Chapter 14: Demos + Presentations
Chapter 15: Create Momentum
Chapter 16: Time Lines
Chapter 17: Negotiation Levers
Chapter 18: Content and Resources
Chapter 19: Referrals
Chapter 20: Building a Prospect List
Chapter 21: Outbound Prospecting
Chapter 22: Qualifying Inbound Leads
Chapter 23: Upsell and Cross-Sell
Chapter 24: Social Plays
Chapter 25: Trade Shows and Conferences
Chapter 26: Playbook Glossary
Chapter 27: Meeting Planning and Debriefing
Chapter 28: Deployment and Continuous
                 Improvement

Future ClozeLoop Books
As of November 2019, we have several books in the works that will be released in the coming months. Be on the lookout for:

- C.O.A.C.H.ing Salespeople
- Triangle Customer Success
- Triangle Selling Scenarios: An Advanced Application of Triangle Selling
- Financial Modeling for Startups
- Business Acumen for Salespeople
- And many more…

APPENDIX B: ADDITIONAL RESOURCES

ClozeLoop is a sales, marketing, and sales enablement agency based in San Francisco, California.

In each of our books, we lay out the very frameworks, science, fundamentals, and processes which we employ in our consulting engagements to generate successful outcomes for our clients. We believe in open-source sales intelligence and want readers to be able to immediately apply the insights from these pages without having to hire more employees or consultants. We love the ever-evolving nature of the selling profession and it's our hope that other smart practitioners and executives will build upon the fundamentals of Triangle Selling and share their insights with us.

We welcome feedback and questions. Please connect with us on LinkedIn and shoot us a message.

The ClozeLoop Engagement Model

ClozeLoop engages with our clients through:

Sales Skills Assessment: A twenty-minute online assessment where we evaluate the sales skills of a team across ten categories. We have specific assessments for sales development reps (openers), account executives (closers), sales engineers (pre-sales technical resources), and sales managers.

Sales M.A.T.H.: A guided executive-level quantitative exercise that begins with top-line revenue goals and then examines the health of the sales organization relevant to its ability to meet or exceed targets. We model Metrics (measure the things that matter—OKRs, KPIs), Alignment strategy (revenue simulations to clearly indicate where vulnerabilities exist), Timelines (cadence of review and performance reporting), and Horizons (long view of revenue targets with leading and lagging indicators and milestones).

Sales Enablement Assessment: A study of a company's current sales enablement ecosystem, challenges, and opportunities, including all departments that directly or indirectly impact revenue.

Triangle Sales Training: Multi-role onsite training for Triangle Selling.

Triangle Success Training: Customer success is the key to recurring revenue, and churn can kill growth. Triangle Success training is not just sales training adapted to customer success but, instead,

built specifically for those who nurture customer relationships and have responsibility for retention, renewal, and upsell of existing clients and customers.

Triangle Management Training: Frontline sales management fundamentals for Triangle Selling teams to develop accountability, coaching, mentoring, hiring and engagement, and leadership skills.

Triangle Certification: Rigorous program for managers, sales enablement professionals, and independent consultants to be able to coach, develop curriculum, train, and reinforce Triangle Selling in their own organizations or with their clients.

Triangle S.H.A.R.E. (Demo) Certification: A rigorous program for companies in which product demonstrations are a key step in their sales process. This certification increases the conversion rate from the demo stage and creates velocity toward disqualification or closed business.

Triangle H.I.R.E. Training: Built for managers, H.I.R.E. training certifies those responsible for building sales teams in Hunting for sales talent, Interviewing effectively for selling roles, Rubric development for hiring success, and Evaluation of

the candidate. When sales hiring is systematized, measurement and predictability occur.

Playbook Development: Develop and deliver a sales playbook that includes actionable sales tactics to ensure that all salespeople have an easy way to access the best plays for any specific selling scenario.

Triangle A.I.M.: The Actionable Insights Map augments a sales playbook with the words, phrases, and sentences that a sales team needs to be effective in conversation with their prospects. Fortified with internal knowledge, customer evidence, external analysis, and solution positioning, this product puts relevant sales-ready language at a salesperson's fingertips.

Online Training: Many of our modules are available online, either in their standard format, or they can be customized to your team.

Thank you for purchasing *Hiring, Onboarding, and Ramping Salespeople.* We wish you tremendous success in your sales endeavors. If we can be a resource in your growth, we welcome the conversation.